Prentice Hall's *Basic Ethics in Action* series in normative and applied ethics is a major new undertaking edited by Michael Boylan, Professor of Philosophy at Marymount University. The series includes both wide-ranging anthologies as well as brief texts that focus on a particular theme or topic within one of four areas of applied ethics. These areas include: Business Ethics, Environmental Ethics, Medical Ethics, and Social and Political Philosophy.

Anchor Volume

Michael Boylan, *Basic Ethics*, 2000

Business Ethics

Michael Boylan, ed., *Business Ethics*, 2001

James Donahue, *Ethics for the Professionals*, forthcoming

Edward Spence, *Advertising Ethics*, forthcoming

Environmental Ethics

Michael Boylan, ed., *Environmental Ethics*, 2001

J. Baird Callicott, *Ojibwa: An Environmental Ethic*, forthcoming

Lisa H. Newton, *Ethics and Sustainability*, 2003

Mary Anne Warren, *Obligations to Animals*, forthcoming

Medical Ethics

Michael Boylan, ed., *Medical Ethics*, 2000

Michael Boylan and Kevin Brown, *Genetic Engineering*, 2002

Rosemarie Tong, *New Perspectives in Healthcare Ethics*, forthcoming

Rosemarie Tong and Reggie Raymer, eds, *New Perspectives in Healthcare Ethics*, forthcoming

Social and Political Philosophy

R. Paul Churchill, *Global Diversity and Human Rights*, forthcoming

Seumas Miller, Peter Roberts, and Edward Spence, *Corruption and Anti-Corruption: An Applied Philosophical Study*, forthcoming

Deryck Beyleveld, *Informed Consent*, forthcoming

Please contact Michael Boylan or Prentice Hall's Philosophy & Religion Editor if you would like to propose authoring a title for this series!

D0209302

BASIC ETHICS IN ACTION

Ethics and Sustainability

Sustainable Development and the Moral Life

LISA H. NEWTON

Fairfield, Connecticut

Prentice
Hall

Upper Saddle River, New Jersey 07458

Library of Congress Cataloging-in-Publication Data

Newton, Lisa H.,
  Ethics and sustainability : sustainable development and the moral life / Lisa H. Newton.
    p. cm.
  Includes bibliographical references and index.
  ISBN 0-13-061796-2
   1. Environmental ethics. 2. Sustainable development. I. Title. II. Basic ethics in action
GE42 .N47 2003
179'.1—dc21

                                            2001058061

Acquisition Editor: Ross Miller
Editorial Assistant: Carla Worner
Editor-in-Chief: Charlyce Jones-Owen
Marketing Manager: Chris Ruel
Production Editor: Judith Winthrop
Manufacturing Buyer: Brian Mackey
Manufacturing Manager: Nick Sklitsis
Cover Design: Bruce Kenselaar

This book was set in 10/12 Palatino by DM Cradle Associates
and was printed and bound by R.R. Donnelley-Harrisonburg.
The cover was printed by Phoenix Color Corp.

 © 2003 by Prentice-Hall, Inc.
Upper Saddle River, New Jersey 07458

Printed in the United States of America

10 9 8 7 6 5 4 3 2 1

ISBN 0-13-061796-2

Prentice-Hall International (UK) Limited, *London*
Prentice-Hall of Australia Pty. Limited, *Sydney*
Prentice-Hall Canada Inc., *Toronto*
Prentice-Hall Hispanoamericana, S.A., *Mexico*
Prentice-Hall of India Private Limited, *New Delhi*
Prentice-Hall of Japan, Inc., *Tokyo*
Prentice-Hall Asia Pte. Ltd., *Singapore*
Editora Prentice-Hall do Brasil, Ltda., *Rio de Janeiro*

*To my children, in hopes that
they will inherit a
better and more beautiful world*

Contents

Preface: Converging Streams

Since the advent of environmental philosophy—sentimentally dated to the publication of Rachel Carson's *Silent Spring* in 1962 and actually in existence since the first Earth Day in 1970—we have wanted to join the swift-flowing pragmatic and political streams of environmentalism with the broad river of ethical theory, especially in its "applied" mode. My previous work, in both ethics and environmental philosophy, positions me well to attempt such a confluence. I would not be working alone: The courses that such a joining would take have been emerging in the literature (especially in the pages of the journal *Environmental Ethics*) for several years. Michael Boylan's invitation to me to contribute a work on Environmental Sustainability to his Basic Ethics in Action series broke through the hard shell of my laziness and set me to work on bringing the streams together.

I believe that this volume is the first attempt at tracing the two streams to their juncture and mapping the course of the river from that point forward. I am grateful to Michael Boylan for goading me into action on the subject, very grateful to Rocky Mountain Institute for permission to quote at length from their publication, *Natural Capitalism*, and infinitely grateful to my family and colleagues for their patience as this work ground on to its completion.

Lisa H. Newton

Introduction:
What Do We Mean
by Living "Sustainably"?

The purpose of this essay is to explore the ethical implications of the notion of "sustainability," a word sufficiently new in the language that it still puzzles my spellchecker. It is new in our thinking, too, especially at the most fundamental levels of our ethical thinking. We now acknowledge that we have, and should have, positive values, a positive orientation, toward the natural residents of our world. We acknowledge that from those values flow duties: From the valuing of any object follows a duty to protect and preserve it. The values that "environmental sustainability" requires us to adopt, however, are different from our other values. They center not on existing particular human beings (the members of our families), nor on human institutions (community, the church, or the nation), nor yet on present human conditions or relationships (the poor, the public or common good, or the shareholders of the corporation). The objects of value for this concept are primarily future generations of human beings (sufficiently future as not to be identifiable with any set of gametes now existing) and the natural non-human environment itself. The perspective of environmental sustainability requires that we ask ourselves how each interaction with the natural environment will affect, and be judged by, our children in the future. A Native American tradition requires those who would use scarce resources to consider their actions from the perspective of those seven generations from themselves. That seems to be a convenient benchmark. Throughout this book, we will be thinking seven generations in the future, about 210 years from now, sometime after 2200 A.D. Keep that in mind.

Let us begin with some rough definitions. Our first problem is "sustainability" itself, for it must encompass the notion of change over time and the notion of the maintenance of the system without change.[1] It is certain that the traditional models of "development," which always entail the conversion of natural landscapes to farmland, and farmland to cityscapes, cannot be sustained. Can we adopt a more subtle notion of "development," something more and less than (economic) growth, the proliferation of goods and services for the "happiness" of human beings—something that could endure forever or at least for as long as the human species is here to sustain it? In this book we will argue that we surely can, and must, if only in order to remain true to a vision of human flourishing that goes beyond enjoyment of goods and services. An ethic that can sustain the best that is in us while empowering us to live in harmony with the natural environment will be the major exploration of the first chapter.

Our notion of sustainability is drawn in part from *Our Common Future*, Gro Harlem Brundtland's Report from the World Commission on Environment and Development meetings published in 1987.[2] It requires that we use our world in a way that will not detract from the future—the seventh generation's—ability to derive the same benefits from similar activities. We must walk lightly on the earth, so lightly as to leave the least possible footprint. That requirement creates difficulty for the notion of "sustainable development," because "development" has always meant expansion of the human footprint. Can it mean something else, compatible with "sustainability"? Can it, for instance, come to mean the refinement of human existence, to include sufficient material goods to maintain life and free the human mind and attention from the demands of survival, in order that humans might work for the betterment of the world in general and the human species in particular? That sounds terribly earnest. Could the freedom include the chance to enjoy leisure, the beauty of nature, the slow evolution of friendship, art and music and philosophy? This notion of "development" would take some arranging. At the end of such development, the "developed" nations of the North would consume, on balance, much less in the way of material goods and far less energy; the less developed nations of the world would consume far more in the way of material goods, enough so that famine and mass pestilence would be a distant memory, and all nations together would become partners in search of the higher possibilities of human nature.

The "long haul" of the title is the time between now and the seventh generation from now. We will be dealing, in what follows, with the political and economic activities of a variety of public actors, including governments, publicly held corporations, and nongovernmental organizations (NGOs), especially those that articulate environmental missions. The tendency of governments is to bend all efforts to the next election; the tendency of corporations is to focus all attention on the next quarterly report; and even the NGOs have to worry about imminent judgment points, fundraising deadlines, and media attention. Our focus in this book will have to be entirely different, and the tension between the present practices of the political actors and the demands of environmental sustainability cannot be avoided. If we are to serve the seventh generation, we will have to think in terms of centuries of elections, quarterly reports, and capital campaigns.

The value commitments of this book begin with the value of personal integrity. Persons do not live very long, and it may seem paradoxical to derive a value that will not materialize until the seventh generation upon the choice of a personal lifestyle for individuals living today. Yet we can only act in the present, and we can only act from the character that we have developed to this point. The assumptions essential for this account, spelled out in Chapter 1, amount to what Michael Boylan has called the "Personal Worldview Imperative": "All people must develop a single, comprehensive and internally coherent worldview that is good and that we strive to act out in our daily lives."[3]

From personal integrity we will derive the other values we need for the long haul: wisdom (including sensitivity to natural processes), courage (including patience), temperance (including frugality), justice (including respect for that which is other than ourselves), love or fidelity (including care and compassion), community, simplicity, humility, and above all responsibility, accountability, a disposition to carry out effectively stewardship of that which has been placed in our care. The first chapter will attempt to provide a context for environmental virtue, as part of a demonstration that only virtue ethics will permit any worthwhile environmental ethic. Fidelity and community will emerge as central virtues, alongside the traditional wisdom, courage, temperance, and justice, as we attempt to demonstrate that the person who would live a caring life in community lives in contradiction if he or she lives in violation of environmental sustainability. Our relationship to natural processes will be the focus of the second chapter, bringing attention to the humility needed to attend to them and the wisdom to discern them. We will conclude that there are ways (some of them new but none of them surprising) in which we can dramatically improve the ways we relate to the earth. Stability, simplicity, and stewardship will be the focus of the third chapter, in which we show that concern for sustainability logically entails a life of voluntary simplicity that reinforces personal integrity at crucial junctures. The ability and opportunity to take responsibility for objects of concern, some integrated pattern of goods and duties, seem to be central to living a good human life. A short conclusion will sum up the argument and attempt to provide some current applications.

NOTES

[1]At one point this essay was to be entitled "Ethics and Sustainable Development," which is indeed an essay in contradiction. "Sustainable" means (at least) "maintaining equilibrium in the long term" and "development" means (at least) "progressive irreversible change," and we are surely dealing with an oxymoron, a contradiction in terms. (Favorite oxymorons include "jumbo shrimp," for example. Other sources put "military intelligence" in this class, not to mention "business ethics.") See Wolfgang Sachs, "Sustainable Development and the Crisis of Nature: On the Political Anatomy of an Oxymoron," in Frank Fischer and Maarten A. Hajer, eds., *Living With Nature: Environmental Politics as Cultural Discourse,* New York: Oxford University Press, 1999.

[2]Gro Harlem Brundtland, 1987.

[3]Boylan, Michael, *Basic Ethics,* Upper Saddle River, NJ: Prentice Hall, 2000, p. 27

chapter one

Morality: Environmental Ethics as Virtue

The first task is to outline an understanding of the individual moral life, life in accordance with a Personal Worldview Imperative, and to show its logical relationship to environmental sustainability. For reasons having more to do with the flow of the argument than with the demands of the logic, we will start with *sustainability*. For a provisional definition, subject to refinement as the argument progresses, we will understand a community, economic system, or other human activity to have reached sustainability when it *can be maintained profitably and indefinitely, without degrading the systems on which it depends.* (For systems that do not include "profit" in their criteria of success, parallel terms may be used: fruitfully, for instance, or productively, or successfully.) For how long? "Indefinitely" means, at the maximum, that there are no foreseeable circumstances in which some limiting resource—fuel, natural materials, land, human intelligence—will fail, and doom the system to failure. Given the uncertainties of this world, that may be too much to ask. Let us adopt the criterion with which we started: No practice shall be regarded as "sustainable" unless it can be continued without degrading the environment that nurtures it through the *seventh generation* from its initiation. Some examples will help; they will give us reference points to clarify the rest of the discussion.

"Sustainable" practices come easily to mind. The establishment of a public library, for instance, founded on the civic responsibility, intelligence, and generosity of the generation that established it, will only increase those resources in the time, however long, in which it flourishes; therefore the public library is a sustainable institution. "Unsustainable" practices are also identifiable. By way of contrast to the library, for instance, our problems with casinos and other practices profiting from gambling, pornography, and the like, have mostly to do with the possible erosion of the civic basis necessary to sustain practices at all. (The objection may not be a good one; Monaco, for instance, has survived for centuries on gambling.) Organic gardens are sustainable, for they take nothing from the land that they do not replace (when run properly), and they add nothing to the land that could hurt it, now or in the future. The pesticide-dominated agriculture of the 1950s is not sustainable; the target insects rapidly evolve into pesticide-resistant strains, while the birds and other natural predators of the target insects are destroyed by the poison. The small businesses that grew in traditional small towns of the agrarian society were sustainable for generations, since they supplied just enough of a needed product (tools, shoes) while sustaining and training the people who would carry on its production in the future. The big-box stores sprouting in the countryside are not sustainable; by dooming all the small shops in the region to failure, they ensure the depopulation (or impoverishment) of their market, and thereby its disappearance. Government subsidies to the displaced persons in the area may keep the market viable for some time, but a practice that must be maintained by government subsidies can hardly be characterized as "sustainable." Highly selective lumbering in old-growth forests is sustainable—the occasional old-growth tree and an adequate selection of new-growth trees can be removed for milling into usable lumber without hurting the forest at all (just as human beings can donate a pint of blood every few months without suffering harm). "Tree farming," the practice of obtaining pulp timber from wide tracts of fast-growing trees that are cut and pulped at maturity, is not sustainable; all the nutrients that entered the trees from the soil are cut down and carted away, and the soil is left too thin to grow anything after three or four crops.

We should distinguish at this point the microcosmic and macrocosmic perspectives on sustainability. The sustainable practices previously mentioned are sustainable in their own microcosms, that is, looking only to the purposes for which they were founded. The macrocosms in which they flourish—the energy use of the library, for instance, or the land use of the organic garden in a very overpopulated nation—must eventually be part of any final judgment on sustainability. We will get to the macrocosm later in this work.

Our approach to sustainability varies from the usual practice of the field. The subject of sustainability is usually approached through the areas in which modifications must be made if it is to be attained, that is, through the *contexts* of sustainable activity. A text on agriculture will focus on those crops, chemical additives, and techniques of cultivation and rotation that will best preserve the land while giving us an acceptable yield of product. A text on economics will focus on the means and measures to ensure that resources will continue to be available in the future. A text on law and regulation will describe particularly exploitative practices that must be restrained. Such limited focus is entirely appropriate. If environmental sustainability in development is desired (however various authors define it), it should not matter to us whether it is achieved by strictly enforced law, powerful economic incentives, or the sudden realization on the part of all parties to the situation that only through continual attention to the environmental consequences of their actions can the natural foundations of their lives be preserved. (That last motive is, quite honestly, the least likely.) Sustainability is an end, and for most purposes it remains for us only to specify the means that will effectively achieve it. In this normative context, motives are not particularly important, save as they can be influenced to produce more effective action.

But for our purposes, we will have to go considerably beyond this bare means–end nexus—we are talking, after all, about living an ethical life, about satisfying the Personal Worldview Imperative[1]—to develop a single, comprehensive, and internally consistent worldview, judged to be good and to be practical, adopted as our own and lived out in our daily lives. No adjustment of means to the end of "sustainability," by the external motivations generally available to us, will even accomplish that end, let alone give us a life to live in accordance with a consistent worldview. We will be arguing that sustainability is a steady state of the soul, as well as of the natural world external to the soul, observed as steadfastness and experienced as serenity. We will also be arguing, as corollary, that the commitment to live sustainably, in harmony with the natural environment, is necessary for the coherence of that worldview; without it, the self lives in contradiction.

The substance of the argument of this chapter has three parts. In the first, we argue that no combination of available political "means" to the "end" of sustainability in economic activity will be effective in attaining that end. (That is not to say that sustainability in economic enterprise is not technologically possible. It is. The technological possibilities will be discussed in Chapter 2.) The incentives and regulations available to us—to all our governments, at any level, in any part of the world—are at best sea anchors in an everlasting hurricane, slowing the pace of assured destruction, with no possibility (even logical) of ultimate reversal. In short, we are going to have to adopt an entirely new approach to preserving the environment and harmonizing human fulfillment with natural systems.

In the second part of the argument, we argue that no combination of happiness-seeking and rule-abiding can orient the human life to a proper relationship with the environment. And if those, the two major ethical orientations of the modern Western world, are not useful to our purposes, we shall have to revert to the classic analysis of the ethical life as a life of "virtue," of an attempt to achieve within the life as lived an excellence of relationship both among the parts of the self and with the outside world.

In the third and concluding part of the chapter, we will argue that this orientation to virtue will permit the description of a fulfilled life that is also compatible with environmental sustainability.

WHY WE WILL NOT ACHIEVE SUSTAINABILITY THROUGH PRESENT MEANS

If *sustainability* is taken as the goal, what are the ordinary paths to attempt to reach it? The two major approaches to achieving sustainability in the economic realm are through punitive regulation and through incentives. One motivates a donkey to move, traditionally, either by striking him on his rear with a stick, creating pain that can be relieved only by motion (and the assurance of a repetition of the pain should he stop), or by suspending a carrot from a stick in front of his nose, creating the possibility of pleasure that can be obtained only by the same motion. That is the role of the government. Legislatures and regulative bodies create sticks through regulations to which are attached sanctions for non-compliance (usually financial sanctions), and carrots through incentives (also financial, usually in the tax structure) for desirable behavior.

When the public goal is to reduce the degradation of the atmosphere by pollution from power plants, for instance, laws will specify the maximum permissible emissions of certain kinds of pollutants, public officials will monitor the power plants, and fines will be levied against the power company if the pollution is found to be in excess of that maximum. To this stick is added the general motivation to obey the law out of civic duty: it is against the law to emit more pollutants than the stated maximum, and every citizen ought to obey the law.

A more enlightened approach to cleaning the air—more enlightened because more likely to be successful—makes sure that the incentive to think about reducing pollution, and to act on any productive thoughts, resides in anyone who has anything to do with the polluter. Federal and state tax incentives reward the companies for decreasing the pollution; if the emissions decrease, their taxes are reduced—the greater the decrease, the greater the reduction—thereby encouraging the managers to think very hard about reducing emissions. If they have any sense, and a surprising number of them do, they provide a schedule of monetary awards for any employee who thinks up a good way to reduce the pollution. Now they have all the brains in the company working on the same problem, maximizing the chance of success.

To the financial carrot is added the general motivation to be a good neighbor, and contribute to the general good of the city by avoiding degradation of the air we all must breathe. It has been observed, however, that "good citizen" motivations—motivations to be a law-abiding and generous neighbor—are seriously ineffective without the financial sticks and carrots of government action.

But in any larger context, the entire stick-and-carrot approach is ineffective in reaching real sustainability. For the moment, let us stay with power plants. While they are burning fossil fuels, they will emit certain predictable waste products. If the combustion process is inefficient, the waste products will include products of incomplete combustion of hydrocarbons, essentially soot. The air will be thick with black floating specks that leave oily smudges where they land. People will choke; a pall of filth will lie over all the city. The condition was not uncommon in the cities of the nineteenth century, in Europe and in the United States. In Pittsburgh, into the 1950s, headlights were needed at noon to navigate through the middle of the city. (Those were steel mills, not power plants, but the pollution is the same.) But we can do much better than that now. Scrubbers remove all but traces of the soot. Chemical processes can even remove most (but not all) of the oxides of nitrogen and sulfur that form naturally when the native coal is burned, oxides that form acid rain in the atmosphere. Smokestacks no longer belch the clouds of black smoke that entombed the industrial cities.[2] Of course, emissions remain; there is no doing anything about the greenhouse gases, especially carbon dioxide, that are the chemically necessary product of any combustion of hydrocarbons. But much progress has been made.

Surely all this is a victory for environmentalism, and a move in the direction of perfect sustainability? Not. For the population of the nation has increased, by 13 percent in the 1990s alone.[3] More importantly, the demand for power from each individual has increased astronomically. All these computers and fax machines need electricity, as do hair dryers, microwaves, electric clothes dryers, and water heaters. The newer buildings in which we live need central air conditioning, which was a rarity only 40 years ago. As we discover new technologies and conveniences, the demand for power rapidly increases in the most developed countries. Across the world, the situation is dramatically worse; an awakening cohort of societies in what is called "the developing world" are discovering that they cannot join the "developed" world in its agreeable habits of consumption without vast increases in their use of power. For them, all the incentives are on the side of greater use of power, and worries about pollution will take second place. The result of these changes, despite claims that we are succeeding in "cleaning up pollution," is that even if we lower the amount of pollution per unit of energy produced to the minimum technologically possible, the absolute amount of emissions will continue to rise due to the huge increase in total demand.

We do not have a governmental decision procedure that could change that result. In any world—first, second, third, developed, developing, East or West, North or South—the public decisions must and will be made according to the present perception of the public good, that is, the good of the present public. Because we take that statement to be analytically true, it might be worthwhile to parse it. The first assumption is that however the influential voices are selected to determine each decision—maybe only a few of the ruler's family, maybe an electorate with universal suffrage—they must be present living voices. The seventh generation will not vote. The second assumption is that all intentional action is directed at some perceived good,[4] and that humans are markedly inaccurate in perceiving goods at any distance from their own. The third assumption is that all our theories of justification of public decision—resting as they do on individual liberty, democratic process, and distributive justice—must bring us back to the interests of present persons and only present persons unless (and it's an unlikely unless) all present persons have a sufficiency of the goods of this world and are willing to see goods set aside for persons not yet in existence.

The immediate consequence of that analysis is that all incentives and regulations are inherently severely limited. How could it be otherwise? If there are tax incentives (or better yet, tradeable pollution quotas) in place to lower emissions, we will lower emissions as far as possible, but in response to rising demand for energy, we will also build new plants. They will emit the lowest amount of polluting substances possible, but as the number of plants increases, the absolute amount of pollution will increase. The tax incentives can do nothing to keep the demand for power down, and in fact, by taking away the strong disincentive provided by a plant pouring out greasy black smoke, they may remove barriers to increased demand.

Can we make laws, ordinances, and regulations to lower the *absolute* amount of emissions into the air? We could try. But we are limited by technology, which will not take us close to zero emissions. We cannot legislate new technology. Even in the realm of forbidding and enforcing, which we can legislate, recall that what legislatures can do, legislatures can undo, and will, when circumstances and political pressures change. When there is enough power for all consumers, regulations can forbid expansion of plants, insist that older plants lower their emissions one way or another or shut down, and even, in times of prosperity, subsidize experimentation with newer "renewable" forms of energy. When there is not enough—and as I write, California is discovering what "not enough" means in these power-hungry times—then new plants will be brought on line as rapidly as possible, and if environmental regulations seem to be getting in the way of the power supply, the regulations will be scrapped. That is political reality.

Let us place ourselves in the shoes of the administrator who is trying to control pollution—not just in the United States but across the world—and see what the picture looks like from his perspective. There may be small and temporary victories; pollution significantly lowered at one plant, in one state or country, for awhile. But the variables the administrator cannot control—population growth and demand growth per unit of population—render every victory hollow, and foretell inevitable defeat. Sustainability cannot be attained, and while every victory is temporary, every defeat is permanent, irreversible.

The same scenario could be repeated in any field of interest to the environmentalists. "Suburban sprawl" can be controlled by careful zoning regulation, as long as there is sufficient political will to maintain it. Let that political will waver, as it will as soon as expanding prosperity makes the green fields of the countryside attractive as new subdivisions, and no history of maintenance of greenbelts will stand against it. Once the land is lost, it is lost for good. "Deforestation" can be halted in the ancient forests, for a while, by vigorous activism, political courage, and enlightened policies to find alternative industry for areas that have lived for centuries on logging and milling lumber. But no matter how many administrations support the halt, the one administration (it may hold office right now) that permits logging in the old forests will end the effort forever. Once those trees are gone, they are gone for good; we cannot grow 1000-year old trees. Further, if the groves have been clear-cut, the rains will wash away the soil of centuries' accumulation, and no forest will grow there ever again. Every preservation project is like the battle to save the ancient forests. In the "give and take," the "compromise," of political decisions, preservation sometimes wins and sometimes loses, but every victory is only a moment to prepare for the next battle, and every defeat is irreversible.

Incentives to prevent pollution, or to preserve environmental goods, have no more future than environmental regulation. They may be the best available stopgap measure to slow the destruction of the natural world, but by their nature, they can work only as long as polluters or despoilers find it profitable to seek them. As long as the incentive is worth more than the market value of ignoring it—as long as the tax incentive for restricting certain kinds of emissions is larger than the cost of the controls—some power companies will choose to control the emissions. When the advantage disappears, or turns negative, the company no longer has any reason (nor, if publicly traded, any right) to follow environmentally sound policies. And the public cannot raise the cost to the taxpayers indefinitely.

Both the stick approach and the carrot approach, then, are ultimately self-defeating. They can only trade on what is marginally profitable or politically acceptable right now. Given the history, and the directions of all the lines projecting into the future, all our environmental efforts along traditional lines are only slowing what is silently conceded to be the inevitable destruction of the natural world. In very practical terms, a new approach is needed.

From our perspective, the search for a sustainable personal morality, there is a more serious problem. The problem is, whether the system is based on the carrot or the stick, it makes nature the adversary of the human. In the creation of incentives for environmentally sound behavior, nature is the merchant across the table in the marketplace. We are trying to make a deal, a deal that will preserve most of everyone's interests. We are trying to make the protection of nature worth the other merchant's while. With enlightened self-interest as the touchstone, we hope to find a balance that will keep all merchants as happy as possible. Given that humans keep multiplying and natural resources do not, no balance will be satisfactory for long. By way of contrast, in law and regulation, nature is the spoiled darling of the elite, protected by laws and trust funds that forever interfere in human enterprise. Every homeowner hates the environmental laws that forbid him to modify the "wetlands" newly discovered on his property. Every citizen rapidly learns to hate the laws that require him to deposit bottles here, cans there, newspapers over yonder, in some endless round of coolie labor that (we suspect) leads all items to the same landfill in the end.

Nature will not survive as our adversary, nor will any moral orientation that makes it an adversary prove sustainable in us. Ultimately, the only moral consciousness that will last will proceed from a personal worldview, directed to the behavior of the person himself for himself—the behavior that best expresses the life he lives because, having learned what is best for himself, he wants to live that way. Only when the preservation of nature is part of the way we want to live will the "adversary" aspect of environmental protection be done away with.

THE SEARCH FOR A PERSONAL ETHIC: TWO STANDARD ANSWERS AND ONE BEYOND THEM

We will need to approach environmental policy in some new and different way. We can start from no better place than the search for a personal ethic, a way of life that is good to live in itself. By the Personal Worldview Imperative, we must create such an ethic. The literature is rich with candidates for such a worldview (including several that suggest that ethical beliefs are not even intelligible, let alone true or important). We will confine ourselves to those that are normally presented for our use in texts that deal most immediately with environmental problems—the literature of applied or practical ethics and the nascent field of environmental studies. In these fields, the moral orientations that are most commonly proffered as justifications for policy and obedience to law are Utilitarianism, set forth with admirable clarity by John Stuart Mill in his 1861 book of that name,[5] and Kantian formalism, set forth by Immanuel Kant in his 1785 *Groundwork of the Metaphysics of Morals.*[6]

Utilitarianism

"Utilitarianism" as the name for an ethical theory, or principle, was first used by Jeremy Bentham in his 1776 *Fragment on Government*. In his *Introduction to the Principles of Morals and Legislation*, 1781, he defined the principle as follows:

> By the principle of utility is meant that principle which approves or disap-
> proves of every action whatsoever, according to the tendency which it appears
> to have to augment or diminish the happiness of the party whose interest is in
> question: or, what is the same thing in other words, to promote or to oppose
> that happiness.[7]

In determining the best course of action, then, we work out the probable consequences of each of our options, and choose that option with the probable
best outcomes for all concerned. Such reasoning is called "consequentialist,"
or "teleological" (from the Greek *telos*, or goal). In theory, as a limiting possibility on the low side, the "party whose interest is in question" might be
only the agent who acts; in this case he would consider only his own interest,
in a framework known as "hedonistic egoism." The "party" often expands
to include the agent's family, his community, his nation, and as a limiting
case on the high side, the entire human race. Mill defines the principle in
much the same way:

> The creed which accepts as the foundation of morals, Utility, or the Greatest
> Happiness Principle, holds that actions are right in proportion as they tend to
> promote happiness, wrong as they tend to produce the reverse of happiness.
> By happiness is intended pleasure, and the absence of pain; by unhappiness,
> pain, and the privation of pleasure.[8]

If "happiness" can mean no more than pleasurable consciousness, as felt by
the experiencer, then that person alone has the authority to say whether it is
present or not. "I am happy," or "I am unhappy (in pain)," on Bentham's
understanding, is *incorrigible*, that is, it refers to an entirely internal state, and
no one has the right to deny or challenge it. The speaker may be lying, but
he cannot be mistaken. The unit of happiness is a moment of feeling happy—
an instant of pleasurable consciousness. That simple understanding of happiness allows Bentham to go on to discover the common good by simple
addition and subtraction, the "felicific calculus."[9] The greater good of the
community, or the community interest, can stand against the interest of the
individual only with the authority of a larger number of individuals.

> The community is a fictitious *body*, composed of the individual persons who
> are considered as constituting as it were its *members*. The interest of the com-
> munity then is, what?—the sum of the interests of the several members who
> compose it.[10]

J.S. Mill recognized the complexity of the concept of happiness, and developed a far more nuanced version of it, based on comparisons by knowledgeable experiencers. Thus if you, who have experienced on a regular basis
grand opera as well as town softball games, and I, who know only the soft-

ball games, are set the task of determining which activity should be encouraged by federal funds, I will have to defer to you, for you can say for sure whether or not the opera exceeds the game in enjoyment. This qualification takes into account the common experience of the educated, who find themselves weighing the numerous kinds and degrees of "pleasures" open to them, and often, because they can conceive so much better, end up failing to find pleasure in what is really there. Mill acknowledges and accepts this drawback of too much experience.

> It is better to be a human being dissatisfied than a pig satisfied; better to be Socrates dissatisfied than a fool satisfied. And if the fool, or the pig, are of a different opinion, it is because they only know their own side of the question. The other party to the comparison knows both sides.[11]

Mill also recognized the necessity of modifying Bentham's simple calculus to determine what should be done in any situation. It isn't just that we do not have time, every time an occasion to act presents itself, to figure out what act will have the best consequences in the long run. It is that we are generally expected to follow rules, and that in the long run, "obeying the rules" will have good consequences (and "disobeying the rules" will have bad consequences) on our character and on the world, far beyond our poor power to predict. Rules are made from the general tendencies of actions; society is best served by adherence to the rule.

> . . . we must not consider the action as if it were single and insulated, but must look at the class of actions to which it belongs. The probable specific consequences of doing that single act, or forbearing from that single, or of omitting that single act, are not the objects of the inquiry. The question to be solved is this—If acts of the class were generally done, or generally forborne or omitted, what would be the probable effect on the general happiness or good?[12]

This understanding of utilitarianism, generally known as "rule utilitarianism," puts a two-step procedure where Bentham had only one. To determine whether or not an act is good, look to the rule governing it; to determine whether the rule is good, look to the consequences of general obedience to it. "Act utilitarianism" would ask us only to look to the consequences of the act, immediately and in the long run. Most of us are rule utilitarians. (It could be argued that "rule utilitarianism" is incoherent; if in any given case we could prove that an act of breaking a generally good rule will have better consequences *in all respects, in the long run, taking everything into account,* than any rule-abiding alternative, then it would be irrational to argue for obeying the rule. Rule-utilitarianism is therefore a shortcut mechanism, increasing the probability of achieving the best possible consequences.)

Mill also allowed more complexity in the notion of "happiness," which has meanings other than simple felt pleasure, absolute or relative. An alternative understanding of "happiness" is from welfare economics, referring to the satisfaction of the objectively determinable physical, social, and psychological interests of a person. On this understanding, a recovering drug addict is "happier" than he was when on drugs, even though the intense pleasure of the drug experience is no longer part of his life. A claim on the part of the active addict when high, or alcoholic when drunk, or manic-depressive in his manic stage, to be "happy," is not, in Mill's position, incorrigible, but can indeed be challenged by anyone in a position to know better. Recent economic theory tends to resolve the two into "preference": In a free market situation, given the resources to exercise options among purchases repeatedly, over a long period of time, what product does the agent actually buy? This newer understanding of "happiness" as "satisfaction of preferences" has a strong advantage: Whatever the individual may *say* to the pollster, or priest, or politician, about what really makes him "happy," in the marketplace he votes with his dollars, so we find out where he will *in fact* commit scarce resources. That information is worth a great deal to those developing products for the market, and is one reason that there is such a close relationship between utilitarian theory and economics.[13]

But the newer definition has several disadvantages. The first, to be taken very seriously in any context that takes ethics seriously, is that where dollars are the only ballot, the poor have no vote. You get to express your preferences in the marketplace only to the extent that you have resources to commit. Second, in cases of acknowledged medical distortions of judgment (as in drug or gambling addictions), the victim may well commit all his resources, including resources he does not have, for purposes that are not under his control. Third, we have not yet decided, as the market has, that the present state of human preference, addictions aside, is in any way normative; we do not know that people cannot learn to prefer other things than they do, nor especially, that they cannot learn to prefer many fewer things than they do. Fourth, human desires are more malleable than Bentham or J. S. Mill ever suspected. We do not have to buy J. K. Galbraith's "dependence effect"[14] in its entirety to conclude that cultural influences often dictate what kind of material desire, in what quantity, is socially acceptable. Utilitarianism will be of only limited value.

The fifth disadvantage, especially crucial for our purposes, is that people who do not yet exist cannot commit resources to that which is not for sale. We can buy toys for our children. But the seventh generation cannot buy anything, and with the best will in the world, we cannot buy intact rainforests for those of that generation, although we think that as adults, the children of that generation will appreciate a rainforest just as much as our children appreciate the video games we buy them. The seventh generation gets to express neither feelings of pleasure, claims of rights, or market preferences, yet somehow decisions have to be made for them. Those decisions will not participate in the free market economy in any way that Adam Smith would understand.

But there is a further, logical, difficulty in using any utilitarian approach to ethics for a personal ethic in harmony with the environment. Utilitarianism requires a specification in advance of the limits of the sphere of moral concern. Jeremy Bentham, as we recall, defined the principle of utility as "that principle which approves or disapproves of every action whatsoever, according to the tendency which it appears to have to augment or diminish the happiness of the party *whose interest is in question*,"[15] telling us nothing about how many should be invited to the party. Mill, as above, assumed (but did not prove) that all human beings were included in the calculation and none others. There is no logical reason to reach beyond the human species, and therefore no real reason to include the natural environment.

But we can, by extension, include the higher animals, if we wish, and this possibility is unique to utilitarianism. The extension is possible on the justification of their developed nervous systems. If their nervous systems are sufficiently like ours, then we may—yea, must—assume that they experience pleasure and pain just as we do. Because the basis of consideration and rights for the utilitarian is the ability to enjoy happiness and suffer pain, it contains within it a foundation for the movement known as *animal liberation*, or *animal rights*. Jeremy Bentham, founder of Utilitarianism, was the first to draw the obvious conclusion.

> The day may come when the rest of the animal creation may acquire those rights which never could have been witholden from them but by the hand of tyranny. . . . .What . . .is it that should trace the insuperable line [between human and brute]? Is it the faculty of reason, or perhaps the faculty of discourse? But a full-grown horse or dog is beyond comparison a more rational, as well as a more conversable animal, than an infant of a day, or a week, or even a month, old. But suppose they were otherwise, what would it avail? The question is not, Can they reason? Nor Can they *talk?* But, *Can they suffer?*[16]

If a thing cannot suffer, it cannot possibly claim, under utilitarianism, to have the right to have its interests taken into account, for it has none; its life cannot be better or worse no matter how circumstances change. The smallest mouse has interests; the largest rock does not. As philosopher Peter Singer argues, in an article provocatively titled, "All Animals Are Equal,"

> If a being suffers, there can be no moral justification for refusing to take that suffering into consideration. No matter what the nature of the being, the principle of equality requires that its suffering be counted equally with the like suffering—in so far as rough comparisons can be made—of any other being.[17]

It does not follow that pigs will vote, or lambs go to school without the teacher having a right to put them out, any more than the assertion of equal rights for men and women entails a man's right to an abortion. But certain practices, Singer asserts, will surely have to come to an end: the ruthless wastage of animals in research on drugs, cosmetics, and all manner of toxins, and the cannibalism inherent in the eating of the flesh of our nearest relatives. (Chimpanzees, for instance, are eaten for dinner in Africa. Their DNA corresponds 98.5% to our own. Even if we restrict the notion of cannibalism to the eating of humans, that makes those diners 98.5% cannibals.) Clearly the thoughtless cruelty and tormenting of animals by humans for amusement, either privately or in public spectacles such as bullfights, would have to stop; in most civilized nations such practices are against the law now. But for Singer, they should be forbidden not because humans should not be coarsened by the chance to be cruel, but because the animals have a right not to be so treated, even as do we.

Not all utilitarians make the extension into animal rights, although for consistency's sake, perhaps they should. But a defense of animal rights will not take us into an environmental ethic of sustainability, much as we might want it to. Let us return to this point when we consider the environmental ethics as a whole.

The Kantian Alternative to Utilitarianism

For purposes of developing a moral life, Immanuel Kant's theoretically fascinating work on ethics boils down to a redirection of attention, from consequences (or tendencies) of acts to the nature of the act performed and the motives of the person performing it. Action is right, for Kant, when it is done in the belief—and on account of the belief—that it is the right thing to do. The goodness of the act resides in the decision of the agent to obey the moral law, to fulfill his duty, rather than in the consequences of the act, actual or foreseen. This is what is meant by his opening assertion, that "[n]othing in the world—indeed nothing even beyond the world—can possibly be conceived which could be called good without qualification except a *good will*."[18] He denies any originality in this claim; ordinarily, we regard a person as "good," or "having acted rightly," if he did what he clearly saw to be his duty, even if the consequences, through no fault of his own, came out badly. We may attach all sorts of values to external objects and to desirable states of affairs—"power, riches, honor, even health, general well-being, and the contentment with one's condition which is called happiness"—but whatever sorts of goods they may be, they are not moral goods. (Kant primly warns that possession of all those good things might lead to "pride and even arrogance" unless conjoined with a good will.[19]) Our moral approbation is reserved for those who do what is right, whatever their inclinations and whatever the consequences. To reason from rule, as Kant insists, is therefore to reason not from consequences, as utilitarianism does, but "deontologically" (from the Greek *deon*, duty), as opposed to teleologically.

The agent must not be entirely unmindful of the consequences, of course; many (most, possibly all) duties envision some consequences. Consider the famous dictum that Kant derives for the moral guidance of our actions, the first formulation of the "categorical imperative": "Act only according to that maxim by which you can at the same time will it should become a universal law."[20] This is not the Golden Rule, "Do unto others as you would have them do unto you," an essentially subjective rule that asks you only to put yourselves in the shoes of the person with regard to whom you are acting. (The Golden Rule can be shown to yield some very strange results in certain structured situations, for instance when a judge exercises discretionary power in sentencing criminals. Do we really want all judges to hand down the lightest possible sentences on vicious and depraved criminals, on the grounds that if *they* were vicious and depraved criminals awaiting sentence, that's what *they* would want?) The categorical imperative requires that you generalize the rule upon which you are acting to all moral agents; can you will that everyone should reason as you have reasoned, to the performance of this action? Should all people act from the motives and duty you have acted on? What would happen if everyone did this?

Kant's appeal is obviously to consequences; in that sense, his theory was never "non-consequentialist." It is very difficult to see how anyone might derive a morality for the real world without taking into account the way that world works and the effects that human action will have in it. Like the utilitarians, he prescribes actions that have desirable tendencies as the subject of the rules. The difference between these very different systems lies in the moral and intellectual springs of the individual action. Once a general class of acts (say, promise-keeping) has been established, and subscribed to by the community of moral agents, then consequences and circumstances do not modify the duty. It is this proviso that separates Kantian deontology from Mill's rule-utilitarianism. For Mill, the way we establish the rule, "we should keep our promises," is by examining the general consequences of promise-keeping, on the one hand, and more particularly, the consequences of failure to keep our promises. Having discovered the goodness of kept promises (we will not bother to list them) and the badness of broken ones, Mill concludes that promise-keeping is good, and adopts it as a rule. If circumstances come up, of course, that make it *very* unwise to keep a particular promise, then we are dispensed from the rule.

For Kant, the goodness of the act in general is contained in its definition; I do not have to take a survey of all cases of promise-keeping or truth-telling to determine that one ought to keep them or tell it. The act of promising contains in it the duty to keep it; if "promise" has any meaning at all in the language, then it should be kept. Similarly, when I speak, and make any claim, I am attesting to the truth of that claim. If it is not true, I have denied what I have, by speaking, asserted, and have contradicted myself. Lying can never be right; the duty to keep promises can never be dispensed.

Can Kant get us closer to a duty to preserve the natural world? It seems not. Unlike utilitarianism, which can at least consider the happiness of the higher animals, Kant does not orient his philosophy to the results of action, whether for happiness or unhappiness, but to the act itself, reasoning, willing, voluntarily acting. For Kant, it is analytic that an act subject to moral description is one for which the agent can (and must) take responsibility. But we have never found it useful, or possible, to hold animals "responsible" for their "voluntary" acts. The notion of moral agency seems to be restricted to human beings. Kant's human-centered limits become even clearer in what he calls the "second formulation" of the Categorical Imperative, or "practical imperative" "Act so that you treat humanity, whether in your own person or that of another, always as an end and never as a means only."[21] This moral ideal is limited to humanity; morality, for Kant, may not extend (save by sentimentality) beyond the human species.

Kant goes on to put forth a third formulation of that Imperative—to act as a legislator in a kingdom of ends. This mysterious kingdom, could it contain lives other than human? We will return to this possibility.

The Search for a Land Ethic

Neither utilitarianism or Kantianism will take us into sustainability. Moral reasoning from human "preferences" cannot take us the whole distance to the seventh generation; laws and regulations are weak reeds on which to lean the preservation of the world. Bentham focused on the happiness of the human race (or at best the higher mammals), Immanuel Kant, unless read very broadly, expected his Categorical Imperative to include only moral agents—those who were capable of conceiving of a maxim for action and willing it. But the point of environmental ethics is precisely to extend the sphere of moral concern to an indefinitely (not infinitely) large community of living things, with principles of action that cannot always be described as "rational." What would an ethic that extended to the land look like?

Presumably we should start with Utilitarianism, which at least got us to a sympathetic appreciation of the putative rights of higher mammals. But animal rights do not take us very far. The first suspicions that the protection of individual animals might be incompatible with the protection of the environment were raised by Aldo Leopold, in his occasional essays combined and published posthumously as *A Sand County Almanac and Sketches Here and There*.[22] In one of his Sketches, from the days when he was a government hunter in Arizona and New Mexico, he records the moment when he realized that he was doing the mountain no favors in the fulfillment of his wolf-extermination assignment. He and his colleague shot an old she-wolf, and reached her

> in time to watch a fierce green fire dying in her eyes. I realized then, and have known ever since, that there was something new to me in those eyes—something known only to her and to the mountain. I was young then, and full of trigger-itch; I thought that because fewer wolves meant more deer, that no wolves would mean hunters' paradise. But after seeing the green fire die, I sensed that neither the wolf nor the mountain agreed with such a view.[23]

The point had been to save the deer. But in state after state that exterminated its wolves, the deer wasted away, overpopulated, consuming "every edible bush and seedling," every edible tree "to the height of a saddlehorn," and eventually themselves. In the end their bones "bleach with the bones of the dead sage, or molder under the high-lined junipers." Cattle ranchers who exterminate the wolves on their land had best realize the responsibility they have undertaken, to keep their herd down to a size that the range can handle. Unfortunately, the farmer "has not learned to think like a mountain. Hence we have dustbowls, and rivers washing the future into the sea."[24] We try to keep ourselves safe, and to the extent that animals are valuable we try to keep them safe too. Maybe that's the problem: "too much safety seems to yield only danger in the long run. Perhaps this is behind Thoreau's dictum: In wildness is the salvation of the world. Perhaps this is the hidden meaning in the howl of the wolf, long known among mountains, but seldom perceived among men."[25]

Success, in nature, seemed intuitively (and through direct experience) to depend on leaving the natural killing in place. The operation of predators is essential to maintaining the health of the whole ecosystem, the land, and those who would manipulate the land had best remember this. Aldo Leopold is joined in this insight by one of his most faithful interpreters, J. Baird Callicott. Callicott begins by pointing out that when Leopold argued, as he did, that an environmental ethic, a land ethic, extended our categories of moral considerability to the natural world, he really meant the *land*.

> The beech and the chestnut, for example, have in his view as much "biotic right" to life as the wolf and the deer, and the effects of human actions on mountains and streams for Leopold is an ethical concern as genuine and serious as the comfort and longevity of battery hens. In fact, Leopold to all appearances never considered the treatment of battery hens on a factory farm or steers in a feed lot to be a pressing moral issue. He seems much more concerned about the integrity of the farm *wood lot* and the effects of clear-cutting steep slopes on neighboring *streams*.[26]

He takes gleeful note of Leopold's continued carnivorousness, even interest in hunting. How could Leopold continue to hunt? Possibly Leopold was unacceptably insensitive (a judgment not borne out by the evidence), or a hypocrite (then why was he so open about his hunting?), or he did not think that respecting the rights of individual animals had anything to do with respecting the land. That third seems to be the case; Leopold's land ethic stands in a triangular relationship with ethical humanism and humane moralism (the foundation of animal rights) in the animal liberation debate.

The land ethic, Leopold's core environmental philosophy, was set forth in the same set of essays:

> A thing is right when it tends to preserve the integrity, stability, and beauty of the biotic community. It is wrong when it tends otherwise.[27]

Those two sentences comprise the entirety of the famous ethic; they bear examination.

The first and most obvious feature of the land ethic is that it is *ecocentric*. We distinguish ethics, in the field of environmental studies, by the center to which all moral questions are referred. Three centers compete for recognition: the human race, the totality of life, and the earth itself, living and non-living. *Anthropocentric* ethics center on the human, and discover value in nonhuman nature only to the extent that it is valuable in some sense to human beings. That value is not set in advance. For instance, Nature may be valuable to us only as the "raw material," "resources," that we use for our industry—logs for our lumber mills, land for agriculture, fish for the table. Toward the beginning of the 20th century, the major competitors in environmental philosophy were an ethic of pure exploitation (it's here, I want it, I take it), vs. a new ethic of "wise use," set forth eventually by Gifford Pinchot, Teddy Roosevelt's Director of Forestry. In "wise use" it is recognized that the only real value nature has is as a resource, but the resource must be so managed that it will be "sustainable"—available to future generations for their exploitation. Pinchot also conceded that people enjoyed walking in the woods, so he made the national forests a "multi-use" resource, to be used for recreational purposes in conjunction with logging.

In designing the national parks, Roosevelt and Pinchot took a very different approach, planning for the major use to be recreational. The point was to keep the woods, mountains, and spectacular views for the enjoyment of all the people, an approach to nature that came to be called "conservationism." Of course, for the people to enjoy them, the parks must be made accessible, so they have good roads, scenic overviews, and wheelchair ramps. But then, is that really nature, the woods that you are enjoying? Should there not be some beautiful areas left just as they are, just as God and Nature gave them to us? This philosophy, "preservationism," was defended by John Muir, with whom Pinchot got into one of his most famous battles (over damming the Hetch Hetchy Valley to supply water and power to San Francisco). Muir argued occasionally as if he thought the land had a value all by itself, independent of humans, but the burden of his argument was that future generations should have the privilege enjoyed by his own, of seeing this natural beauty as it was. His view did not prevail at the time, but eventually we designated national wilderness areas, off limits to roads and other improvements, for the enjoyment of people possessed of the same passion as Muir's to see the natural world in its natural state. That's four different approaches to management of the natural world; but you will note that they all center on some perceived good for human beings. It should be noted at this point—and it will become crucial later on—that preservationism is supported not just by the hardy backpackers who trek those wilderness areas, but also by a very large number of Americans who will never get there, who just want the woods *there*. There for future generations, there because we owe such preservation to our ancestors, or just there because the soaring forests and the wild rivers are some part of America that is unique to us and that we wish, for that reason alone, to preserve.[28]

The last half of the 20th century saw some experiments with non-anthropocentric centers for valuing. The Animal Rights initiative, for instance, moved the center of gravity from the species *homo* to all sensate life, stopping moral considerability at the point where that life no longer has nervous systems like our own (and therefore presumably cannot feel pain). We may extend the circle of considerability further, to include all that share the mystery of life itself—the processing of energy for growth and reproduction that covers the earth in green foliage and little wiggling things. Such an ethic would be *biocentric*, making the prosperity and continuation of life in all its forms the criterion of what is good. To the extent that human activities poison other life, displace it from its natural habitat and commandeer its resources, the human becomes a criminal in the community of living things, and deserves active curtailment. To take another metaphor for life: Life as we observe it seems to be one living being, a huge organism of itself, sometimes personalized with the name *Gaia*, the Greek name for Mother Earth. To the extent that one species grows without limit—outstripping its role in the organism, displacing other organs, draining resources, exuding toxins—that species is a cancer in the body. It has to come out.

But Leopold goes beyond biocentrism. Let us look at that passage again:

> A thing is right when it tends to preserve the integrity, stability, and beauty of the biotic community. It is wrong when it tends otherwise.

What does it mean? *Integrity* as a human virtue has been used to designate many qualities, but primarily the ability to act always as the same person, in one character. The person of integrity is the goal of character formation, the person we can trust and the person we want to be; we will return to this virtue in humans. In an ecosystem, or biotic community, *integrity* is more difficult to define, if only because it lives, potentially, forever, or as long as the earth shall last, slowly *changing* character as climate and other factors change around it. Humans live only long enough for one maturity; the ecosystem can have an indefinitely large number of them, as it persists through the eons, and no one of them is privileged as the reference community, to which all others are to be compared and found deviant. *Stability* also is a relative term, given something that necessarily changes, if slowly, over time. But given that long-term limitation, stability is the foundation of the biotic community's identity. A stable system will maintain its features in the face of natural shocks. It can survive viruses that all but wipe out a key species; other species will occupy its niche until, given enough time, it returns. It can survive devastating fires, volcanic eruptions, flooding rivers, and hurricanes. While it retains its health, it will come back. *Beauty* is not ordinarily understood as a moral imperative, but then, ecosystems understand morality in a way different from our own. Among living things, that which is *beautiful*, in any but the most jaded understandings, is that which is in the bloom of health. The elements of the visual presentation of natural health—symmetry, proportion, order, not unmixed with sexual attraction—can then be generalized to the proportions, balances, and compositions found in the non-living world, which inform our notion of artificial beauty. The ecosystem that is healthy is beautiful; the ecosystem that has been devastated by toxins and by the destruction of its component species is not. The judgment, in Leopold's understanding, is much more than aesthetic.

But the emphasis is on *community*. The deer, flower, vine, or rippling stream may be beautiful in itself, but the harmony of the system requires that it stay within the balance of the competing species. To preserve the ecosystem—the delicate and beautiful balance of life and death and proliferation that characterizes a working community of soil, plants, rocks, streams, and all the animals that depend on them—it may be a moral requirement to kill white-tailed deer when the population is too high, and equally a requirement to protect and nurture the cruel and murderous predators that like to eat the deer. Depending on circumstances, the "right to protection" may devolve on certain plants, on the trees, or on the (inanimate) waters of the stream itself, threatened by pollution; that right may infringe on the interests of sheep, who would like to graze in the woodlands. The land is to be seen as an organic whole, its parts interdependent, its interests merged into one and superseding the interests of any member of it.[29] This is what we mean by "ecocentric": it is the ecosystem itself, ultimately the ecosystem of the whole natural world, that is the center for value.

The ethical "holism" that Callicott urges does not make a value of "community" as some other entity, beyond the individual beings that make up the ecological community. It simply insists that the being cannot be considered outside of the role that it plays in the community, and that its "right" to protection is not possessed by it as an individual, but only in virtue of that role.

(Hence the pollinators own special status, in view of the dependence of the plants upon their performance of their function; the predators, as above, deserve special consideration; and so forth.) This ethic is genuinely ecocentric, as indicated at least by its unwillingness to make exceptions for *homo sapiens* or for any other species, no matter how cute or intelligent. Where there are too many deer, or rabbits, or people, regard for the biosphere requires that the number be reduced. The conclusion may seem difficult; Callicott draws his warrant from Plato's *Republic*, in which the ideal state is perfectly willing to sacrifice individual lives and relationships for the good of the community.[30]

But then what happened to sentience, or sensibility, as a criterion of the moral, and the capacity for suffering as a condition of moral considerability? Callicott rejects them completely, even going on to point out that in the larger context of ecology, the "pain and suffering" of an individual cannot be easily condemned as bad, if incurred in the pursuit of its normal life.

Where does ecocentricity lead us? Eventually, to an ethic (or perspective) known in the field as "deep ecology," the perspective that takes the earth seriously as a single living organism and single center of value, and condemns humans as hostile to its purposes. The practical consequences of taking deep ecology seriously, including the removal one way or another of most of the human race, are too extreme to contemplate, so very few do. But the position is out there, as a logical extreme of the environmental ethic.

In our search for a personal ethic, where does the land ethic take us? Because we look for an ethic compatible with sustainability (though we have not yet said why), we must take the ecocentric perspective seriously, and attempt to integrate it with a viable personal worldview. By itself, it does not yield an ethic for any but the seriously suicidal; but we will argue in the section that follows that it can be integrated with a full and rational personal ethic to supply one of the meanings of a full human life.

THE NEXT FOUNDATION FOR ETHICS

To review: We intend to develop the notion of a personal ethic that will characterize a fully realized human being and will contain, of necessity, a commitment to the ethic of the land. We want to say what it is to live a full and unified human life in a world under assault. We will make certain assumptions.

The first assumption is that we ought, and normally want, to live logically consistent moral lives. We ought, and want, to live *rationally*, or intentionally, deciding what we shall do and how we shall live according to generalizable rational principles. (If that seems an unwarranted assumption for the majority of the human race, let us put it in the negative: No one capable of understanding the choice would choose *not* to live in accordance with rational choices.)

The second assumption is that we ought, and normally want, to live *good* lives. That is, by whatever ethical standards we have selected (and these do not turn out to be subjective, arbitrary, or infinite in number), we must be able to see our lives as not only logically of one piece but also as aimed toward the Good, in one of its facets, the expression of an ethical worldview. That facet may be truth or the life of the mind (the favorites of the academic profession), justice, healing, beauty, the protection of the poor, the preservation of the natural world, service to God through some religious institution, or the fulfillment of one of many natural or imposed duties (raising one's children, doing one's job). But it must be clearly part of the Good, and all of the moral imperatives we adopt must be consistent with it.

These two assumptions entail one of the primary conditions of the moral life: that we remain open to reasoned criticism of our actions or our lives, from others, or from our own more mature selves. We must remain willing to change our orientations to home in more precisely on that facet of the Good that we have chosen, and have come to understand more completely in the course of our life experience.

The third assumption is that we ought, and normally want, to live *our own* lives. That is, at the end of the reasoning, comparing, and revising, we must make our own choices about what part of the Good we will pursue, and we must recognize them as part of ourselves for which we must acknowledge responsibility. (In newer language, we must take *ownership* of our moral orientations and of the choices that follow from them.)

It is logically impossible that any aspect or facet of the Good is logically incompatible with any other, although the life choices entailed by attention to one of the facets may render sustained attention to the others difficult or counterproductive. In practice, we are often faced with dilemmas of competing goods, or competing evils—situations where all choices open to us have some undesirable result. The existence of irreducible ethical dilemmas has been part of common understanding at least since W. D. Ross' *The Right and the Good*,[31] and these dilemmas dominate the subject matter of professional or practical ethics. The preceding assumptions form the starting point for resolution of dilemmas in personal and public life. When faced with apparently incompatible courses of action, both of which appear to be prescribed by some set of normative forces in my life—family, work, community, law, or religion—I must make the choice rationally (as opposed to arbitrarily or impulsively), morally (as opposed to carelessly or for immediate gain alone), and responsibly (willing to be personally accountable for the choice, the reasons for it, and the consequences of it).

How does the commitment to environmental sustainability follow from the imperative to develop a personal worldview? The best way to explain the connection begins with a standard forced-choice decision tree.[32] (The inevitable oversimplification will be remedied, we hope, in the commentary to follow.)

First, can any personal worldview include the imminent destruction of the self? Apparently not. It is accepted that there are times when people see their own imminent destruction as the only immediate outcome compatible with their commitments and worldviews, and we admire them for their willingness to accept it (one thinks of captured spies, captains of sinking ships, soldiers left to cover the retreat). But the admiration holds only if they held life-affirming commitments and worldviews prior to entering those circumstances, and if arriving in those circumstances was beyond their control. (Those who commit suicide from depression get no credit for their martyrdom.) So a desire to continue in being into the future, to be active and to enjoy life in the future, is part of any coherent personal worldview.

Second, can a personal worldview include only the self? Logically yes, but morally no, and by the terms of the framework of ethics in which we have to work in practice (and in terms of which this series is conceived), it is the moral personal worldview that interests us. Logically, it is possible to be a complete egoist. In practice, it is not, for reasons that need not be rehearsed at this point. We are bound to others, and, being human and therefore inclined to create institutions, to the institutions that we create to formalize and facilitate our duties to other humans. We cannot conceive of ourselves without the forms of family and community that define and bound us. So the personal worldview, being a moral worldview, must take into account bonds of family, community, and the other institutions created to protect and nurture those bonds: church, state, and the multiple institutions of the economy. We may note at this point that by "community" we do not (necessarily) mean the local community, the "village" of Aristotle's *Politics*, the small rural town of American sentimentality (or alternatively, some collection of urban "neighborhoods"). Your community is created in part by you; it may be based on bonds of interest rather than locality, and it may be spread out over the country or (through the Internet) the world.

Putting those two results together, we reach the first obligation of sustainability: *We must desire the continuity of our families and our communities*, if we are to be whole people ourselves. Communities and families ground us in space and time. They contain our records, the history of what we have done, assuring us of our own existence and continuity, and the receptacles for our future actions and existence. It is the community (however designated and circumscribed) that remembers us, holds our past, and therefore can recall us to ourselves; it is the community that expects us in the future, and calls out (when it is working as it should) the very best that is in us. We are always performers on the stages of our kinship, local, professional, or otherwise chosen communities, measuring ourselves by their reaction to what we are and what we do, projecting our future selves in relation to them. As we love ourselves, and are essentially related to one or more communities that we call our own, we must desire their future existence.

The conclusion to this point is transparent: To be coherent persons ourselves, we must commit ourselves to the care and protection of human community into the future. This commitment is known, in the tradition, as the duty of stewardship, and it has a long and honorable history. We could wish that this generation might be more explicit about its commitment to such stewardship.[33] We envy the civic spirit of the towns of the 19th century, who spoke easily, when they built their libraries and their hospitals, of the gratitude of generations centuries in the future, the everlasting renown of their donors, and the unending train of righteous consequences from actions taken in the present. For them, seven generations was the day after tomorrow. But let us note, when they built, they rarely included the protection of the natural environment in their ambit of achievement. As a matter of fact, the speeches that accompanied the dedication of their civic monuments often celebrated the "conquest" of the "wilderness" achieved by their forefathers. How will we ever go from the celebration of community, as a natural and excellent extension of the self, to an ethic of respect for nature?

The answer is in front of us, or, as my students would say, in our faces. We are physical. We are bodies. We are living bodies, like all other species, that co-evolved with all the species on which we depend for food—co-evolved in a world without contemporary sorts of pollution. We tend not to think about air, for instance, breathable air, but we need it. Already there are places on this earth, some in the United States, where people need to carry oxygen. We need unpolluted water, and water does not grow in plastic bottles. (Our food also, plant and animal, requires such water, or we will not be able to eat safely.) Physically, we are part of the flow of nature. But our bonds with nature extend beyond the mindless dependency of bodies on ecosystems. We must not forget that in co-evolving with all other species, we came to recognize them as our own, our partners in life. Only in the last few centuries—no evolutionary time at all for anything larger than a fruit fly—have we lived our lives at any distance from contact with, indeed immersion in, nature. Could it be that our psychological, emotional, lives, are tied to nature quite as much as our lungs are tied to oxygen, for most of the same reasons?

In 1984, Edward O. Wilson of Harvard University advanced the thesis that humans have an innate affinity for the natural world, an affinity so strong as to be a biological need. It is, he argued, integral to our development as individuals, just as it was essential to our development as a species.[34] We are naturally formed to live with, relate to, and protect nature, and when we adopt some course of life hostile to that living, we endanger our lives at a level far too deep for us to understand. Since 1984, Wilson has acquired critics and defenders (most notably among the latter Stephen Kellert of Yale), but the thesis has quietly gained in adherents and in practical applications (for instance, in placing patients recovering from surgery near windows looking out on plantings).[35] This literature brings us full circle. We arise physically out of nature, and in nature we find our home and our sustaining basis. There is no way that we will find sustainability in our communities unless we recognize that, whatever its moral basis otherwise, the natural world is part of our community, and we cannot do without it. Therefore in considering the bounds of the moral self, the "other" that must form the object of our moral life, the natural world is necessarily included.

VIRTUE ETHICS: FROM ARISTOTLE TO LEOPOLD

Let us review. We began with two requirements for an ethical system. The first requirement, the essential requirement, is that it permit an integrated life, a life that we would agree is good. The second requirement is that it somehow extend to the natural world, and manifest itself in a commitment to the natural sustainability of our practices with regard to that world. We have shown that the two requirements are logically linked—that no ethic for an individual life can logically exclude a commitment to the community in which it arises and flourishes, and that the community is by our nature composed of the land as well as its human residents.

The question, then, is how to derive the ethic itself, the imperatives for living our human lives in community. Utilitarianism and Kantian formalism will take us some distance—to regard for our long-range material interest, for instance, and to obedience to environmental regulations made for the common good—but they fail us as soon as major lifestyle changes are entailed by their calculations, and they cannot be integrated with any personal moral imperative. Can we do better? In fact the philosophical tradition yields another tradition that may do what we need. Going back to the ancient Greeks, there is an orientation known as "virtue ethics" or "aretology" that supplies a method of ethical reasoning based not on the act—the goodness of the objective or its rightness according to rule—but on the nature and motive of the actor. With this orientation, we reason neither teleologically, toward desired consequences, nor deontologically, from established duties, but "ontologically," that is, from our nature itself. Because this approach to ethics was all but abandoned when utilitarianism and its critics took the stage in the modern period (at least until Alasdair McIntyre revived it),[36] we will take a moment to track the central lines of reasoning peculiar to virtue ethics. To avoid retracing steps later in the argument, and to clarify the virtue ethics approach by illustration, we will consider how these ancient versions of virtue ethics might be applied to the development of an environmental ethic.

We may start with Plato, to whom all succeeding philosophy may be regarded, according to Whitehead, as footnotes. For Plato, as represented by his centrally important work *Politeia* (*The Republic*), the operant virtues seemed to be (he assumed, never proved) wisdom, courage, temperance and justice.[37] What might these mean? Plato is not specific, so we need not be. By wisdom, we may understand all knowledge relevant to good decision making in the field to which the wisdom is to be applied. For Plato, that field was statecraft—the science of governing human beings in states so that both humans and the state will flourish. For good political governance, Plato patiently proved, the statesman must above all be able to control himself—to keep his own greed, lust, and fear under control. After that, he must understand the strengths and limitations of other human institutions—the family (against which he mounts a devastating critique in the *Republic*), the farming community (of which he paints a hilarious portrait), and the larger state. Environmental governance covers the same levels as political governance, but with a different science. For environmental governance—of self, corporation, community, or nation—the appropriate knowledge is ecology, the science of ecosystems, the understanding of how they work and what they need to flourish. As governors of nature, we need to know how nature works, our own nature and that of the nonhuman world, just as Plato's philosophically trained rulers needed to know how human beings and human institutions work. To bring the application into the academy, we may say that wisdom includes the biological science of ecology quite as much as psychology, since we must learn to adjust our institutions to the needs of the natural as well as the human world. To bring the application into action, we may say that wisdom is what Leopold means by "thinking like a mountain."

By "courage," Plato was quite clear that he did not mean the tendency to go flying off to deeds of derring-do in battle. (On the contrary, he based one of his flawed states, the "timocracy," on that tendency.) Courage is standing fast, holding on, remaining unchanged in the face of fear and desire; courage is patience and perseverance in the face of obstacles. For many of the important contexts of human action, we do not need dramatic deeds; we need patient endurance and careful discernment of the proper time to act. In the complex international affairs of the 20th century, we do not need to be reminded that just such patience is often the virtue most needed by the military, and by the others who must decide policies of war and peace. It is also necessary in the implementation or execution of a broad range of governmental policies, and never more so than in environmental governance. Face to face with nature, patience and perseverance is of the utmost importance. Nature does not work according to human deadlines, does not produce on cue, and often seems to require service without reward. (Nature also provides services without payment; some of these will be the subject of the next chapter.) Those who have engaged themselves in the effort to preserve nature will be well aware of the requirements. If I fight valiantly to save the forest, my only reward, at the end of a successful battle, is that the forest is still there, as it was before, unchanged, for now. Nothing has actually been "gained." If I win, I will have to fight again, and again, sooner and later. If I lose once, there will be nothing left to fight for. Surely patience, perseverance, a willingness to resume the battle without losing heart, and a residual cheerfulness in the face of adversity, are among the most valued of environmental virtues, and they are all part of courage.

Temperance is the virtue of proper prioritizing, keeping things in proportion and in their proper place. Specifically, when it comes to human passions and desires, temperance means restraint of wanting, recognition that there are values of higher place than the immediate satisfaction of desire. It is by this virtue that we are able to keep economic demands—for richer investments, higher paying jobs, more things to decorate our lives, more expensive and energy-consuming modes of living and transporting ourselves—from overwhelming our wisdom and discernment of the proper way to live. Plato saw temperance primarily as restraining unworthy political ambition in the state, and unworthy material ambition in the human soul. The reward of temperance is the contentment that comes with satisfaction with our own position and possessions. (In that, later schools of philosophy followed him; both Epicureanism and Stoicism taught that the key to happiness for ourselves was serenity, that is, to desire no more than that which we already have.[38]) Temperance may also tell us when we are asking too much for ourselves of a limited system of resources, and when we must leave things in place for future generations, but that would be to add a consequential consideration that Plato does not need. Temperance, like the other virtues, is its own reward, in the peace of mind, in the freedom from gnawing desire, that it imparts to the temperate life. From an environmental perspective, it is not difficult to see that the temperate life, if lived by all, might be the best possible protection for the environment.

Justice is also restraint, but of a different kind. Justice is the recognition that each part of a complex system has its role, and requires non-interference; each part must do its own job and not be tempted to move in on the others. Justice, for Plato, is the virtue of letting the other virtues flourish in their own domain. Under the category of justice we can understand the inchoate (and sometimes incoherent) calls for "animal rights," "ecosystem rights," and "respect for nature." The nonhuman world demands our recognition of its ends, acknowledgement of its legitimacy, and right to seek its own flourishing generally without our interference, just as do our human neighbors.

An understanding of the Platonic concept of justice is not rendered easier by our insistence on reducing all moral claims to assertions of "rights," or "entitlements," within the Anglo-American legal system that has grown up in the Common Law since the 16th century. To attribute to any thing a "right" in our system is to endow it with "interests," that is, ways in which it can fare better or worse (so far so good) but also to endow it with the ability to assert and protect those interests in a court of law, by itself or through a proxy. All living things can have interests, for they try to preserve their lives, grow, and reproduce. Plants do those things as clearly as do animals; rocks do not. But the ability to defend those interests in court as "rights" is very problematic. The notion of rights was invented for human beings, and every human being in our system has, somehow, the ability and power to defend his own interests. If he cannot do that himself by virtue of minority or any other incapacity, the court will appoint someone to do that for him. In the end, the state is the guardian of all incompetents who have no other guardian. That takes care of the humans. But the fabric of "rights" does not stretch easily over nonhuman life. Lawmakers are unsure (and unwilling) to appoint appropriate representatives of the interests of the land. Courts are a poor place to fight their battles, and the language appropriate to courts confuses their issues. To see how the Platonic notion of justice protects the biosphere, we must take a step back, see the natural world as a whole as a nested set of cooperating functions (as Plato saw human society), and develop from that understanding our duties of restraint from encroachment on its proper domains.

From this very limited sketch of the Platonic account of the virtues, then, we can already find possible applications in an environmentally sound life—applications that Plato, of course, never made. Aristotle, similarly oblivious to environmental duties, nevertheless defined the good human life, strictly from the human point of view, in a way from which environmental duties can be discerned (not derived). His argument, in the *Nicomachean Ethics*, is well known. He begins by surveying the various understandings of "good" and "happiness," and links happiness to virtue, defined as that condition in which the fulfillment of function is maximally possible. What is human function? As the "function" of any thing is that which it performs uniquely well, and only humans have the capacity to reason, human function must be action in accordance with a rational principle. If we add that the good human life must be the life of that function performed excellently, as well as possible, we can then define the good life for the human being as "an activity of the soul in conformity with excellence or virtue, and if there are several virtues, in conformity with the best and most complete."[39] Aristotle goes on to point out that the definition entails action; "virtue" is not a characteristic, like beauty or a good digestion, that might belong to a person no matter what he in fact did. This active life is experienced by the virtuous person as pleasurable, for each person derives pleasure from what he loves. If he loves justice, he will derive pleasure from just acts.

> In most men, pleasant acts conflict with one another because they are not pleasant by nature, but men who love what is noble derive pleasure from what is naturally pleasant. Actions which conform to virtue are naturally pleasant, and, as a result, such actions are not only pleasant for those who love the noble but also pleasant in themselves. The life of such men has no further need of pleasure as an added attraction, but it contains pleasure within itself.[40]

Aristotle seems to have little interest in the life of self-deprivation or strict adherence to rule that we often associate with the word "virtue." The good life, once attained, is at once "good as well as noble . . . in the highest degree," but more than that, it's fun. It is also the most stable and durable of lives, and should luck turn against the virtuous man, he will take misfortune with better grace than those who have not cultivated such stability of soul. We find in Aristotle's treatment of the good life one of the first instances of the insight that informs Western morality at its best to this day: that it is what a person does, not what happens to him by chance, that makes him happy or wretched. If it is activity that determines life, "no supremely happy man can ever become miserable, for he will never do what is hateful and base."[41]

Why do so few people seem to enjoy this sort of life? Aristotle suspects that they did not acquire the proper habits as youngsters. The virtues do not "exist by nature," as he understands the phrase, "for nothing which exists by nature can be changed by habit." His examples are unforgettable:

> For example, it is impossible for a stone, which has a natural downward movement, to become habituated to moving upward, even if one should try ten thousand times to inculcate the habit by throwing it in the air [a good assignment for his graduate students]; nor can fire be made to move downward, nor can the direction of any nature-given tendency be changed by habituation.

And his conclusion interesting:

> Thus, the virtues are implanted in us neither by nature nor contrary to nature: we are by nature equipped with the ability to receive them, and habit brings this ability to completion and fulfillment.[42]

Unlike our natural abilities—vision, hearing, and the like—we do not have the virtues, and then manifest them. First we manifest them in the appropriate behavior, then we acquire them. We learn them. We start out by obeying rules; Aristotle does not say whether we obey them for fear of punishment, for desire of reward, or because we have some mystical respect for rules. Probably all three. But the point is, they are good rules, and so when we get into the habit of acting as they command, we have acquired good habits.

> Lawgivers make the citizens good by inculcating good habits in them, and this is the aim of every lawgiver; if he does not succeed in doing that, his legislation is a failure. It is in this that a good constitution differs from a bad one.[43]

Obeying the rules, we practice the virtues. It is not enough just to do the actions; once we have the bare bones of the rules down, we must strive to obey them fully, excellently. It is that striving that, in the arts, distinguishes a good performer from a bad one when both have learned by the same rules. Becoming a good person is like acquiring an art:

> The same holds true of the virtues: in our transactions with other men it is by action that some become just and others unjust, and it is by acting in the face of danger and by developing the habit of feeling fear or confidence that some become brave men and others cowards. The same applies to the appetites and feelings of anger: by reacting in one way or in another to given circumstances some people become self-controlled [temperate] and gentle, and others self-indulgent and short-tempered. In a word, characteristics [habits] develop from corresponding activities. For that reason we must see to it that our activities are of a certain kind, since any variations in them will be reflected in our characteristics. Hence it is no small matter whether one habit or another is inculcated in us from early childhood; on the contrary, it makes a considerable difference, or rather, all the difference.[44]

We will revisit this passage and wonder whether the advertising and merchandising directed at our children from the earliest years onward is really as harmless as we tend to assume.

But for the moment let us stay with Aristotle. The point of this exposition has been the portrait, at least in outline, of the good human being—the one who will act appropriately, nobly, justly, with gentleness and self-control, in any circumstances in which he finds himself. The right act is not the point, nor the act best calculated to achieve the most beneficial object, but the character from which the act springs:

> An act is not performed justly or with self-control if the act itself is of a certain kind, but only if in addition the agent has certain characteristics as he performs it: first of all, he must know what he is doing; secondly, he must choose to act the way he does, and he must choose it for its own sake; and in the third place, the act must spring from a firm and unchangeable character. . . . In other words, acts are called just and self-controlled when they are the kind of acts which a just or self-controlled man would perform; but the just and self-controlled man is not he who performs these acts, but he who also performs them in the way just and self-controlled men do.[45]

There is in humans, then, a fundamental indeterminism: Humans are not good by nature, so we have to pay attention to how we bring them up; humans are not bad by nature, so we need not resign ourselves to the predatory behavior of those in power; humans can live noble and self-controlled lives and enjoy them thoroughly, if we will but bend our communities to the task of habituating people to be strong and self-controlled rather than weak and self-indulgent. We are not justified in confidence or despair, and we are without excuse. Compare a contemporary commentary on the recent sequencing of the human genome:

Take, as an example, the various learning mutations that have been discovered in fruit flies and subsequently in mice and people (chromosomes 2 and 16). These are found in genes that are central to memory and learning, many of them part of the CREB (cyclic-AMP response elements binding protein) system in the brain. The mutations reveal that every time a person learns something, he has to switch on some of these genes in order to lay down new connections between brain cells. . . . If genes are at the mercy of behavior, but behavior is also at the mercy of genes, then our actions can be determined by forces that originate within us as well as by outside influences. . . . This makes it deterministic and responsible, but not predictable.[46]

(By "deterministic," the author intends to distinguish learned behavior from chance events.) Aristotle apparently has genomics on his side; our behavior may spring from genetically determined patterns, but those patterns are laid down by habitual behavior.

Virtue ethics has able advocates in the realm of environmental philosophy. Geoffrey Frasz, for one, explored the possibility that virtue ethics might provide a valuable foundation for an environmental ethic. We may start with his definitions:

An *environmental virtue* refers to a mean between two vices [one of several Aristotelian approaches], qualities the possession of which will partially enable a person to lead the environmentally good life. The good for humans in this case is living in harmony with nature. I focus on the virtues of character rather than the intellectual virtues, realizing though that a full account of environmental virtues has to consider both kinds. (A worthwhile exploration in this area would be to examine just what is involved in "thinking like a mountain" [what we have called "wisdom"]).[47]

Frasz points out that virtue ethics is peculiarly suited to the demands of environmental ethics because it considers not individual acts and their consequences but long-term patterns of action. The problem with our actions with regard to the environment is precisely that we do not know, when we do them, what the consequences will be. Over a large range of environmental action, we cannot even trust in the goodness of law; by the time we figure out what law would be good to protect the environment, and pass it, it is already too late. To act rightly with regard to the environment, then, we must act from right motive, or right orientation, not from calculation of what law applies or what consequences will flow, for these cannot be known.

Virtue ethics has certain notorious problems. It is unable to give concrete advice to a neophyte in a novel situation ("act as a prudent person would act," you not being prudent, is little help). It has to explain away moral immaturity, although periods of immaturity characterize every virtuous person (recall Leopold's early enthusiasm for killing wolves). And it runs into grave difficulties when it tries to explain its key terms (what, really, would an "environmentally sustainable" orientation to action look like, apart from a history of actions compatible with sustainability?) As Alasdair MacIntyre has pointed out, "virtue," unlike "beneficial action," is always understood as part of a tradition, and when traditions are in the process of rapid change, it is difficult to pin down what will count as virtuous. In the case of an environmental ethic, in fact, its practitioners are often consciously and seriously attempting to change traditions of value.

Yet virtue ethics has certain advantages. Faced with certain egregious assaults on the natural environment, assaults such as clearcuts on the steep slopes of the sequoia forests, or the burning of the oil wells in Kuwait, we surely want to condemn them, but traditional consequentialist or rule-governed moral discourse may not lend the means. What is the consequence of the clearcut or the burning? We may make educated guesses, but because these atrocities have few precedents, in the future available to us to scan, it may be difficult to find any at all. What moral rules were violated? If the redwoods were on the private property of the company that cut them, and if the firing of the wells was an act of war in a belligerency then in process, there may be no rules at all that are not made up at the moment and specifically to condemn, from a perspective not shared by all, assaults on the natural environment. But everyone can understand the virtue ethics approach, as captured by Thomas Hill:

> I want to ask, "What sort of person would want to do [such wanton acts of destruction]?" The point is not to skirt the issue with an *ad hominem*, but to raise a different moral question, for even if there is no convincing way to show that the destructive acts are wrong (independently of human and animal use and enjoyment), we may find that the willingness to indulge in them reflects the absence of human traits that we admire and regard as morally important.[48]

Hill goes on to argue for the centrality of the moral virtue of humility (the opposite of arrogance), and makes the case that from that virtue follow the sensitive appreciation of nature that is prerequisite to desiring to protect it, and the gratitude for nature's beauty that motivates preservation. Frasz differs from Hill on this point, suggesting that what Hill calls "humility" might better be called "openness" to nature—the virtue of proper observation, and of caring about the object observed enough to want to observe properly. Whatever name we give it, the direction of the argument is clear. We seek a description of the excellent human being, one of whose excellence is fidelity to the natural world, and the rejection of arrogance and human superiority is the first step to that life. This excellence is what Leopold incorporated in his recognition that humans are not rulers, but "plain members and citizens" of the natural world.

Frasz' argument is taken up by Bill Shaw, who also adapts Aristotelian ethics to include a duty to sustain the natural environment. For Shaw, this adaptation is a route toward incorporating Aldo Leopold's "land ethic" into standard ethical systems.[49] The development of an Aristotelian treatment of the land ethic requires what is fashionably known as a "paradigm shift," a new way of perceiving the world as well as recognition of new priorities and imperatives in dealing with it.

> Because ecosystems include nonhuman as well as human subjects among its "citizens," Leopold's ethic does indeed demand a reevaluation and a reorientation in our thinking. The object of this process is to bring into harmony these nonhuman and human subjects by bestowing a special status upon those systems exhibiting a *telos* (in Aristotle's terms, a "nature," a "way of being"). A forest, no less than a human, exhibits the capacity for internal self-direction— for growth, for blossoming, for achieving its *telos*—and for that reason forests and other natural systems are respected as citizens in this new paradigm.[50]

The immediate "corollary," of course, is that the human being, no longer master of the land, becomes, as above, "plain member and fellow citizen" with all the rest.

We emphasize that the adoption of a land ethic, and land virtues, is a "paradigm shift," to account for the fact that when we are truly respectful of the land and its natures (its natural objectives, or *teloi*,) we do not have to enumerate duties and enforce laws to bring about appropriate behavior. Right action flows naturally from natural attitudes, arising from the way these things are perceived.[51] Once we know the natural world as a community of purposes, just as is the human world, environmental moral consciousness follows immediately. This is the orientation of "holism": it is the whole biotic and non-biotic natural community that has value, and human preferences cannot be brought in at the end of the analysis to trump the results.[52]

Shaw begins with the suggestion that the search for the Right and the Good—for "knowledge of the good life and right conduct"[53]—is not sufficient for a mature environmental ethic. He turns to Aristotelian "virtue ethics," because in its focus on the attitudes and approach to life of the individual, it leaves open the questions of the limits within which his moral conduct shall be expected—the boundaries of the "morally considerable."[54] As a modern, Shaw has to confront an accusation that would have been incomprehensible to Aristotle: that "virtue ethics" does no more than take the natural tendencies of the natural world and call them "good" without further derivation. Because Aristotle saw the moral universe as essentially a community of purposeful existences, not only of humans but also of all natural objects and all communities, the fulfillment of all those purposes seemed unequivocally good.

But doesn't that just take what *is* (the growth and orderly development that Aristotle observed in the natural world) for what *ought to be* (a natural imperative to achievement of fulfillment and maturity)? This equation has been recognized, since David Hume's *Inquiry Concerning Human Understanding* and G. E. Moore's *Principia Ethica*, to be a logical error, the "naturalistic fallacy."[55] The fallacy would be illustrated by any imputation of moral direction ("ought") to anything that empirically manifests a *telos* (exhibits "striving," or "purposefulness," like a flower leaning away from a nearby tree "in order to reach the sunlight"). Shaw confronts the accusation, and grants the fallacy. If we try, as J. S. Mill does, to derive the (normative) "desirability" of any thing from the (empirical) observation that is "desired," the syllogism is surely invalid.[56] If from the flower's leaning, we proceed further to derive the flower's "desire" for the sun, and therefore the normative requirement of making sure that flowers receive sunlight, we compound the naturalistic fallacy with childish anthropomorphism. But if we take as our endpoint the flourishing of the human being, in some sense the fulfillment of the best of his natural potential, then we have a valid path to that derivation. For human flourishing is only possible in communities, and communities exhibit overriding purposes of their own that are an emergent product of the strivings of their members. Recognition of *teloi*, therefore, endpoints of natural striving for each of the members of the community and for the community itself, creates a common bond within communities, human or extended. For Shaw, the "conscious or unconscious sense of kinship or citizenship that emerges from a recognition of this bond" can be the source and foundation for an environmental ethic.[57]

Then what are the land virtues, for Shaw? The excellent condition of the land, for Leopold, consisted in "integrity, stability, and beauty." The virtues that we must incorporate are those that will foster that condition. Shaw suggests three virtues as central. First, respect for natural communities, for every thing with a *telos*. This virtue, incorporating curiosity, sensitivity, and receptiveness to the needs of the nonhuman, seems to map onto Thomas Hill's "humility" and Geoffrey Frasz' "openness." There can be no doubt that it is hopeless to ask any person lacking this trait to exhibit novel and thoughtful behavior toward the environment (although he may be able to obey rules). Second, prudence, caution, the determination to proceed deliberately and carefully when undertaking action that will impact the environment. Shaw cites approvingly James Heffernan's evaluation of the sensitivity of ecosystems:

> [E]cosystems that are stable relative to characteristic fluctuations or stresses in which they have evolved may not be stable relative to human-induced stress no matter how diverse they are, simply because shifts in the characteristic diversity induced by high technology or large population influxes are not the kinds of stress to which even the most diverse ecosystems have evolved a resistance.[58]

For this reason we must be much more circumspect in entering a natural ecosystem than, say, effecting changes in Disneyland.

The third land virtue that Shaw recommends is "practical wisdom," which, counterintuitively, seems more closely related to justice than to wisdom. "Practical wisdom" is the tendency to honor existing and established needs and relationships, and to balance the claims of each against the others to achieve the best possible solution to the inevitable conflicts. Human interests must not always prevail, as they would in a reassertion of the right of humans to dominate every other species. Human interests must not always yield, as they would in some readings of the "deep ecology" orientation. Balance must be found, and traditionally, it is the role of justice to find it.

Shaw's insight is expanded in a recent article by Philip Cafaro, "Thoreau, Leopold, and Carson: Toward an Environmental Virtue Ethics."[59] Cafaro argues that environmental ethics is seriously incomplete if restricted to tracts on rights and responsibilities and interests; that virtues, exemplified by the lives and teachings of the great environmentalists, constitute environmental morality. The virtues he suggests consist in

1. An appropriate subordination of economic goods to other human goods;
2. Cultivation of scientific knowledge and recognition of its limits;
3. Acknowledgement of the moral considerability of the nonhuman world;
4. Support for the protection of wilderness.

Before tracing that argument, and extracting from their virtues a model for ourselves, let us note that there is an uncanny resemblance to Plato's list in Cafaro's derivation, and since there is no citation, we may assume that the convergence is natural. "Appropriate subordination" of greed and unlimited physical and economic interests is no more than Plato's temperance and Aristotle's continence; scientific knowledge, containing, in Cafaro's version, the recognition of its own limits, becomes wisdom, moral considerability becomes Thomas Hill's "humility," Frasz' "openness," Shaw's "respect," and everybody's "environmental consciousness," the recognition of the legitimate objectives of natural beings. His "protection of the wilderness," flowing immediately from that last, is a species of justice.

Cafaro continues with an interesting review of the lives and work of Henry David Thoreau, Aldo Leopold, and Rachel Carson, as exemplars of environmental virtue. His review of Thoreau begins with the famous passage in which the philosopher describes his chief end in his isolation:

> I went to the woods because I wished to live deliberately, to front only the essential facts of life, and see if I could not learn what it had to teach, and not, when I came to die, discover that I had not lived. . . . I wanted to live deep and suck all the marrow out of life . . . to know it by experience, and be able to give a true account of it in my next excursion.[60]

Cafaro points out that Thoreau's language throughout the work refers to *flourishing, living well*, the language of the virtue philosophers and not the deontologists. To the standard catalogue of moral virtues—sympathy, honesty, justice and generosity (part of Aristotle's canon if not Plato's)—he adds the intellectual virtues of curiosity, imagination, and alertness (paying attention, carefulness).[61] For the construction of an environmental virtue ethics he includes temperance, integrity, sensitivity (respect) for beauty, and most important, simplicity. For Thoreau, it is the virtue of simplicity (understood as a variety of temperance) that makes a life of integrity possible, first, because we are not compromised by "wants" demanding satisfaction, and second, because we are not distracted from our chief end by multifarious pursuits.[62]

Aldo Leopold is most known for his extension of human ethics to the land, for the plea that we regard all of nature as a commonwealth, a community, of which we are but plain members and citizens. But throughout the *Sand County Almanac*, there is a parallel plea, a plea for attention—not to himself but to nature. Our problem, he argues, is that we are blind, we do not perceive "quality in nature." We do not carefully attend, read the signs of what is going on in the land around us, and so we think that there is nothing going on at all, let alone anything worth saving. The quality he refers to, the sensitivity to nature that allows us to see and hear what is there to be seen and heard, to attend to it, to appreciate it, to come to value it, and finally to adopt a commitment to work to protect it—whatever may be its name—is a classic case of an Aristotelian virtue. It is not "there" by nature; we know many people who die without an inkling of it. Yet it can be inculcated by habit, by any systematic and informed exposure to nature. Once you learn to perceive quality, worth, in nature, you cannot forget how, or fail to perceive it. Yet, as performers must practice constantly to perform well, and highly trained professionals practice even more than the learning amateur, this sensitivity is an excellence that can be continually improved. Part of the virtue is the motivation to expand and refine it. It's not an example that would have occurred to Aristotle, but he could not have chosen a better one for his purposes.

As if to complete the Aristotelian agenda, Rachel Carson was planning, when she died, a book on that very inculcation. Tentatively titled *Help Your Child to Wonder*, it was to have dealt with what Aristotle would have called the lawgiver's task, of ordering the child's world in such a way that good habits are acquired.[63] Carson herself was an excellent model of the land virtues, especially of that sensitivity to the beauty of nature, honed through a life of biological research, expressed in bestsellers on the saltwater life of New England. But for her the central virtue was, as with Thomas Hill, humility:

> The "control of nature" is a phrase conceived in arrogance, born of the Neanderthal age of biology and philosophy, when it was supposed that nature exists for the convenience of man . . . .[The] extraordinary capacities of life have been ignored by the practitioners of chemical control who have brought to their task . . . no humility before the vast forces with which they tamper.[64]

And she finished, a few months before her death, full circle to Plato: "We still talk in terms of conquest. . . . I think we're challenged, as mankind has never been challenged before, to prove our maturity and our mastery, not of nature but of ourselves."[65]

How does our contemporary interpretation of "virtue ethics" match up with the Platonic and Aristotelian origins? As above, the parallels are uncanny, with two exceptions. On the parallels, prudence or wisdom—especially as an understanding of science and its limits, and as an understanding of the imperatives of ecosystem management—is virtually identical from Plato to this day, with only a change of field of applicability. Courage, not mentioned by Cafaro, is amply demonstrated in the lives he chooses to use as exemplars: Thoreau defying every convention of a convention-ruled society, Leopold continually crosswise of the people who thought they were managing nature properly, and Carson, weakened by disease, under continual attack from some of the most powerful moneyed interests in the country, staying by her message until her death. Temperance, the containment of material desires, is the first virtue for all the environmentalists. Justice, the virtue of restraint in the presence of other natures and functions, is the keystone virtue of respect for nature. (Integrity, taken as a separate virtue by some of the writers, is assumed as basic to all by the Greeks.)

Two virtues have been added. First, there is the virtue of simplicity, a type of temperance, marked by the strict pruning of material desires and intellectual conceits until the least possible demand is made upon the natural environment. The Greeks would not have been interested in that virtue; the aristocrats who read and wrote philosophy would have associated "simplicity" with the peasants. We may note Socrates' treatment of "the simple life" in the first version of the "ideal state" in the *Republic*, rejected by Glaucon as "a life fit for pigs."[66] (We shall return in Chapter 3 to the development of "simplicity" as a virtue.) The second virtue, from the same source, is humility. Humility means standing back, getting out of the way, yielding place—especially so that there may be time to see what is really going on. The aristocratic Greeks would certainly not have been interested in any virtue associated with their slaves, and indeed it is from the "slave religion," Christianity, that we have learned it. In Plato's description of courage, we can even find praise for pride. But pride is no virtue in contemplation of nature. We need to be humble. We need to learn, and to defer.

If we put the virtues not in the cardinal order suggested by Plato, but in the order of *expanding domains of control*, the concentric circles of community discussed by Baird Callicott, the parallel is even more striking. Virtue, for starters, is regulative. What does virtue regulate?

First of all, virtue regulates the self. What would it be to be a virtuous human being? Here we find the first virtues—temperance, frugality, simplicity—speaking only to the self and its choices about orientations to life.

Second, virtue regulates the family, and all members of the immediate household. These are not all human, at least in the evolved experience of human life. The animals, soil, water, and other natural features of the immediate life of the farm, have been as close and as crucial members of the household as have the parents and children. For the household, central to life and to upbringing, that "careful attention" we keep coming back to is central—love, affection, and a constant willingness to serve and to care for. In Chapter 3 we will call this virtue "responsibility," or "stewardship," and we will discover that it is central to the good human life.

Third, the household extends to the community, or village—the primary locus of human interaction, whether geographical, virtual, or any other type. For this community, wisdom emerges as primary, for the welfare of the community often depends on physical, economic, and political factors that go beyond the household-level experience of its members. The exercise of stewardship in the community requires therefore a commitment to learn what must be learned to protect and maintain it. Included in the interests of the community is the preservation of the environment in which it lives and functions. Here the environmental stewardship responsibilities reach beyond the means of sustenance for the household and extend to the region (its aquifers, its woodlands) in which the community abides.

Fourth, the state requires the exercise of the virtue of "justice." This virtue permits pluralism, the coexistence in peace and fruitful interaction of a variety of moral communities. The commitment to the state is not, save for those appointed to office, one of stewardship. It is, rather, an acceptance of the variety of *teloi* of the human communities that make up the state, and respect for their choices of action. That is not the case with the lands of the state. National lands are the lands of all the citizens severally, not collectively. Those lands are ours to protect, and no collective delegation of responsibility to Departments of Environmental Protection, or Interior, can relieve us of that responsibility. As we must respect the other communities, sometimes distant from us and not sympathetic, that make up the state, so we must protect the ecosystems of the nation, even those we have never seen, for without that protection they will be destroyed.

Finally, the responsibility must be extended abroad. The virtues of wisdom and stewardship here are simply extended to ecosystems in foreign lands that are under attack. There is no doubt that they affect us; justice aside, the rainforests of the earth are major producers of oxygen for the world, and without them we will die. The last years of the 20th century brought home to us the responsibility of the citizens of the world for the environment of the world.

"Virtue" has an unfamiliar, and not altogether pleasant, ring in the 21st century. Yet several of the "virtue ethicists" of the environmental persuasion insist that the life of virtue is a genuinely joyful life. One of the most eloquent statements is from Arne Naess, the famous (or infamous) "deep ecologist:"

> Without a change in consciousness, the ecological movement is experienced as a never-ending list of reminders: "shame you mustn't do that," and "remember, you're not allowed to . . ." With a change in mentality we can say "think how wonderful it will be, if and when . . ." "look there! What a pity that we haven't enjoyed that before . . . ." If we can clean up a little internally as well as externally, we can hope that *the ecological movement will be more of a renewing and joy-creating movement.*[67]

Cafaro admits that "In defending wild nature and asserting its intrinsic value, environmentalists are necessarily proscriptive. Yet the writings of the great naturalists, and our own experiences, tell a story of joyful interrelation with nature. Just as classical virtue ethics provided strong self-interested reasons for treating others with respect—reasons based on a person's concern for his own virtue and flourishing—so an environmental virtue ethics can provide strong grounds for environmental protection."[68]

Conclusion: A Model Worth Cherishing

We may be sure that the personal worldview of a life in harmony with environmental sustainability in all its enterprises is entirely possible for an individual. Right now it is not clear that that model of the moral life, as spelled out in this chapter, is generally possible in the world in which we live. After all, we have lived out our existences in a world in which nature has fallen before the chainsaws, bulldozers, and developers, in which no alternative to the falling of nature has ever been presented. Maybe the defeat of nature is inevitable, necessary for progress, essential for human fulfillment. This chapter has provided no refutation of that possibility.

But we may take this ethic as a hypothesis for an environmentally sustainable orientation to human and natural life, which is at once dutiful—carried on in recognition of our duties to nonhuman nature, perfecting a life in which these duties are unfailingly carried out—but also joyful, lived in full enjoyment of the wonders and beauty of the natural world. The material conditions of the life of virtue here foreshadowed are still unknown, and will be considered in the next chapter. Perhaps we will all have to live as our Puritan or Neolithic ancestors did in order to save the natural world. If so, we have in the preceding sketch the moral framework to adopt an abstemious life of voluntary simplicity. But perhaps that will not be necessary. To the technology of the future we now turn.

NOTES

[1]See Michael Boylan, *Basic Ethics*, Upper Saddle River, NJ: Prentice Hall, 2000, p. 27.

[2]Here's an interesting sidelight. The WPA painters of the 1930s included factories pouring out thick plumes of black smoke in all their pictures of America, not as a disapproving comment on pollution, but as an approving comment on prosperity. I am told that when the first visitors from the People's Republic of China arrived on these shores in the 1970s, they could not believe that our newly regulated factories were actually working, because there were no columns of black smoke arising from them into the blue sky.

[3]Peter T. Kilborn, "Bit by Bit, Tiny Morland, Kan., Fades Away," *The New York Times*, May 10, 2001, p. A1.

[4]Aristotle, *Nicomachean Ethics*, I, 1.

[5]*Utilitarianism*, in Mary Warnock, ed. . *John Stuart Mill: Utilitarianism, On Liberty, and Essay on Bentham, together with selected writings of Jeremy Bentham and John Austin*, New York: Meridian Books, 1962.

[6]Immanuel Kant, *Groundwork [Foundations] of the Metaphysics of Morals*, ed. Lewis White Beck, New York: Library of Liberal Arts, 1959.

[7]Bentham, *Introduction to the Principles of Morals and Legislation*, Chapter I, "Of the Principle of Utility," in Warnock, ed., *John Stuart Mill*, p. 34.

[8]Mill, *Utilitarianism*, in Warnock.

[9]See Bentham, *Introduction to the Principles of Morals and Legislation*, Chapter IV, "Value of a Lot of Pleasure or Pain, How to Be Measured," in Warnock, p. 64ff.

[10]Bentham, in Warnock, p. 35.

[11]Mill, in Warnock, p. 260.

[12]Mill, in Warnock, p. 325.

[13]See, for an extended discussion of utilitarianism in comparison with other ethical theories, Michael Boylan, *Basic Ethics*, Upper Saddle River, NJ: Prentice Hall, 2000.

[14]John Kenneth Galbraith, *The Affluent Society*, Boston: Houghton Mifflin Company, 1958, p. 155.

[15]Bentham, in Warnock, ed., p. 34.

[16]Bentham, *Introduction to the Principles of Morals and Legislation*, Chapter XVII.

[17]Peter Singer, "All Animals Are Equal," *Philosophic Exchange* vol. 1 # 5 (Summer 1974), reprinted in *Animal Rights and Human Obligations*, ed. Tom Regan and Peter Singer, Englewood Cliffs: Prentice Hall, 1976. For the extended argument, see Peter Singer, *Animal Liberation: A New Ethic for Our Treatment of Animals*, New York: Avon Books, 1977.

[18]Immanuel Kant, op. cit., p. 9 [393].

[19]Ibid.

[20]Kant, p. 39 [421].

[21]Kant, p. 47 [429].

[22]Aldo Leopold, *A Sand County Almanac and Sketches Here and There*, New York: Oxford University Press, 1949.

[23]Leopold, p. 130.

[24]Leopold, p. 132.

[25]Leopold, p. 133.

[26]J. Baird Callicott, "Animal Liberation: A Triangular Affair," *Environmental Ethics* 2:311–338 (1980); reprinted in *The Animal Rights/Environmental Ethics Debate*, ed. Eugene C. Hargrove, Albany: SUNY Press, 1992, pp. 37–69, at 39. Callicott later added a sequel, "Animal Liberation and Environmental Ethics: Back Together Again," in *Between the Species* 5:163–169 (1988), not so much a retraction as an exploration of the overlap in logic and interest between the animal rights and ecocentrism schools. The latter essay is also reprinted in *The Animal Rights/Environmental Ethics Debate*, pp. 249–261.

[27]Leopold, pp. 224–225.

[28]Mark Sagoff has argued to this point. See "At the Shrine of Our Lady of Fatima, or Why Not All Environmental Values are Economic," in his *The Economy of the Earth*; also "Nature and the National Idea," in the same volume, especially pp. 139–145. Mark Sagoff, *The Economy of the Earth: Philosophy, Law and the Environment*, New York: Cambridge University Press, 1988.

[29]Callicott, pp. 42–45.

[30]Callicott, pp. 50–52.

[31]W.D. Ross, *The Right and the Good*, Oxford: Oxford University Press, 1930.

[32]Some of this argument parallels the development of the Personal Worldview Imperative in Boylan, *Basic Ethics*, Upper Saddle River, NJ: Prentice Hall, 2000, specifically "Introduction."

[33]Specialized literature on stewardship in the fields of accounting, environmental compliance, and parish management are available, but rarely attempt comprehensive expositions of the whole range of this duty.

[34]Edward Osborne Wilson, *Biophilia*, Cambridge: Harvard University Press, 1984.

[35]See also Stephen Kellert and Edward O. Wilson, eds., *The Biophilia Hypothesis*, Washington, DC: Island Press, 1993; and Stephen Kellert, *Kinship to Mastery: Biophilia in Human Evolution and Development*, Washington, DC: Island Press, 1997.

[36]Alasdair McIntyre, *After Virtue: A Study in Moral Theory*, 2nd ed., Notre Dame, IN: Notre Dame Press, 1984.

[37]Our normal reference here is *The Republic*, in any translation.

[38]See Epicurus' "Letter to Menoecus," collected in *The Stoic and Epicurean Philosophers*, ed. Whitney J. Oates, Modern Library Giant, New York: The Modern Library, 1940, pp. 30–32. The Stoics are possibly best represented by Epictetus, "Ask not that events should happen as you will, but let your will be that events should happen as they do, and you shall have peace." (*Enchiridion* 8), from the same collection, pp. 468–483, at 470.

[39]Aristotle, *Nicomachean Ethics*, tr. Martin Oswald, New York: Macmillan Publishing Company, 1962 (Library of Liberal Arts), p. 17.

[40]Ibid., p. 21.

[41]Ibid., p. 26.

[42]Ibid., p. 33 (all three passages).

[43]Ibid., at 34.

[44]Ibid., p. 34–35.

[45]Ibid., p. 39.

[46]Matt Ridley, "The Year of the Genome," *Discover*, January 2001, p. 53.

[47]Geoffrey B. Frasz, "Environmental Virtue Ethics: A New Direction for Environmental Ethics," *Environmental Ethics*, Fall 1993, 15(3):259–274, p. 259 note 1.

[48]Thomas E. Hill, Jr., "Ideals of Human Excellence and Preserving Natural Environments," *Environmental Ethics*, Fall 1983, 5(3):211–224, p. 212. Cited in Frasz, p. 265.

[49]Bill Shaw, "A Virtue Ethics Approach to Aldo Leopold's Land Ethic," *Environmental Ethics*, Spring 1997, 19(1):53–68.

[50]Ibid., p. 55.

[51]See John Rodman, "Four Forms of Ecological Consciousness Reconsidered: Ecological Sensibility," in *Ethics and the Environment*, Donald Scherer and Thomas Attig, eds., Englewood Cliffs, NJ: Prentice Hall, 1983), pp. 88–92.

[52]Shaw, p. 56.

[53]Susan J. Armstrong and Richard G. Botzler, eds., *Environmental Ethics: Divergence and Convergence*, New York: McGraw Hill, 1993. p. 52.

[54]See Kenneth E. Goodpaster, "On Being Morally Considerable," *The Journal of Philosophy*, 75:308–325 (1978).

[55]See G.E. Moore, *Principia Ethica* (1903) Chapter 1. (Reprinted New York: Prometheus Books, 1988).

[56]*Utilitarianism*, Chapter IV: "Of What Sort of Proof the Principle of Utility is Susceptible," Warnock, *John Stuart Mill* p. 288.

[57]Shaw, p. 54n.

[58]James D. Heffernan, "The Land Ethic: A Critical Appraisal," *Environmental Ethics*, Fall 1982 4(3):235–47, cited in Shaw, p. 65.

[59]Philip Cafaro, "Thoreau, Leopold, and Carson: Toward an Environmental Virtue Ethics," *Environmental Ethics*, Spring 2001, 23(1):3–17.

[60]Henry David Thoreau, *Walden*, Princeton: Princeton University Press, 1989, pp. 90–91.

[61]Cafaro, pp. 6–7

[62]Thoreau, p. 91, cited in Cafaro, p. 7.

[63]Cafaro, p. 11; apparently he got this from Linda Lear's excellent biography, *Rachel Carson: Witness for Nature*, New York: Henry Holt, 1997, mentioned in his previous footnote.

[64]Rachel Carson, *Silent Spring*, Boston: Houghton Mifflin, 1962. Cited in Cafaro, p. 12.

[65]Lear, p. 450, citing "CBS Reports," 1962.
[66]Plato, *Republic*, Book II, 372–373.
[67]Arne Naess, *Ecology, Community and Lifestyle: Outline of an Ecosophy*, Cambridge: Cambridge University Press, 1984. p. 91. Cited in Cafaro, p. 4, note 5.
[68]Cafaro, p. 5.

BIBLIOGRAPHY

Aristotle, *Nicomachean Ethics*, trans/introduction and notes by Martin Ostwald, New York: Macmillan Pub. Co./Library of Liberal Arts, 1989.

Armstrong, Susan J. and Richard G. Botzler, eds. *Environmental Ethics: Divergence and Convergence*, New York: McGraw Hill, 1993.

Bentham, Jeremy, *Introduction to the Principles of Morals and Legislation*, selections, in Mary Warnock, ed. *John Stuart Mill: Utilitarianism, On Liberty, and Essay on Bentham, together with selected writings of Jeremy Bentham and John Austin*, New York: Meridian Books, 1962.

Boylan, Michael, *Basic Ethics*, Upper Saddle River, NJ: Prentice Hall, 2000.

Cafaro, Philip, "Thoreau, Leopold and Carson: Toward an Environmental Virtue Ethics," *Environmental Ethics* 23(1):3-17 (2001).

Callicott, J. Baird, "Animal Liberation: A Triangular Affair," *Environmental Ethics* 2:311-338 (1980); reprinted in *The Animal Rights/Environmental Ethics Debate*, ed. Eugene C. Hargrove, Albany: SUNY Press, 1992, pp. 37-69.

Callicott, J. Baird, "Animal Liberation and Environmental Ethics: Back Together Again," in *Between the Species* 5:163-169 (1988), reprinted in *The Animal Rights/Environmental Ethics Debate*, pp. 249-261.

Carson, Rachel, *Silent Spring*, Boston: Houghton Mifflin Company, 1962.

Epictetus, *Enchiridion*, in *The Stoic and Epicurean Philosophers*, ed. Whitney J. Oats, Modern Library Giant, New York: The Modern Library, 1940, pp. 468-483.

Epicurus, "Letter to Menoecus," collected in *The Stoic and Epicurean Philosophers*, ed. Whitney J. Oates, Modern Library Giant, New York: The Modern Library, 1940, pp. 30-32.

Frasz, Geoffrey B., "Environmental Virtue Ethics: A New Direction for Environmental Ethics," *Environmental Ethics*, Fall 1993, 15(3):259–274.

Galbraith, John Kenneth, *The Affluent Society*, Boston: Houghton Mifflin Company, 1958.

Goodpaster, Kenneth E., "On Being Morally Considerable," *The Journal of Philosophy*, 75:308-325 (1978).

Heffernan, James D., "The Land Ethic: A Critical Appraisal," *Environmental Ethics*, Fall 1982, 4(3):235-247.

Hill, Thomas E., Jr., "Ideals of Human Excellence and Preserving Natural Environments," *Environmental Ethics*, Fall 1983, 5(3):211-224.

Hume, David Hume, *An Inquiry Concerning Human Understanding*, ed. Eric Steinberg, Indianapolis: Hackett Pub. Co. 1977.

Kant, Immanuel, *Groundwork [Foundations] of the Metaphysics of Morals*, ed. Lewis White Beck, New York: Library of Liberal Arts, 1959.

Kellert, Stephen, *Kinship to Mastery: Biophilia in Human Evolution and Development*, Washington, DC: Island Press, 1997.

Kellert, Stephen, and Edward O. Wilson, eds., *The Biophilia Hypothesis*, Washington, DC: Island Press, 1993.

Kilborn, Peter T., "Bit by Bit, Tiny Morland, Kan., Fades Away," *The New York Times*, May 10, 2001, p. Al.

Lear, Linda, *Rachel Carson: Witness for Nature*, New York: Henry Holt, 1997.

Leopold, Aldo, *A Sand County Almanac and Sketches Here and There*, New York: Oxford University Press, 1949.

McIntyre, Alasdair, *After Virtue: A Study in Moral Theory*, 2nd ed., Notre Dame, IN: Notre Dame Press, 1984.

Mill, John Stuart, *Utilitarianism*, in Mary Warnock, ed. *John Stuart Mill: Utilitarianism, On Liberty, and Essay on Bentham, together with selected writings of Jeremy Bentham and John Austin*, New York: Meridian Books, 1962.

Moore, G. E., *Principia Ethica*, Chapter 1. Oxford, 1903. Reprinted New York: Prometheus Books, 1988.

Naess, Arne, *Ecology, Community and Lifestyle: Outline of an Ecosophy*, Cambridge: Cambridge University Press, 1984.

Plato, *The Republic*, tr. Francis Cornford, Oxford: Oxford University Press, 1956.

Ridley, Matt, "The Year of the Genome," *Discover*, January 2001, p. 50ff.

Rodman, John, "Four Forms of Ecological Consciousness Reconsidered: Ecological Sensibility," in *Ethics and the Environment*, ed. Donald Scherer and Thomas Attig, Englewood Cliffs, NJ: Prentice Hall, 1983, pp. 88-92.

Ross, W. D. *The Right and the Good*, Oxford: Oxford University Press, 1930.

Sagoff, Mark, "At the Shrine of Our Lady of Fatima, or Why Not All Environmental Values are Economic," in Sagoff, *The Economy of the Earth*; also "Nature and the National Idea," in the same volume, especially pp.139-145. Mark Sagoff *The Economy of the Earth: Philosophy, Law and the Environment*, New York: Cambridge University Press, 1988.

Shaw, Bill, "A Virtue Ethics Approach to Aldo Leopold's Land Ethic" *Environmental Ethics*, Spring 1997, 19(1):53-68.

Singer, Peter "All Animals Are Equal," *Philosophic Exchange*, Summer 1974, 1 (5), reprinted in *Animal Rights and Human Obligations*, ed. Tom Regan and Peter Singer, Englewood Cliffs, NJ: Prentice Hall, 1976.

Singer, Peter, *Animal Liberation: A New Ethic for Our Treatment of Animals*, New York: Avon Books, 1977.

Thoreau, Henry David, *Walden*, Princeton, NJ: Princeton University Press, 1989.

Wilson, Edward Osborne, *Biophilia*, Cambridge: Harvard University Press, 1984.

chapter two

Technology:
Living Lightly
Upon the Earth[1]

HOW SMALL IS BEAUTIFUL:
SCHUMACHER AND APPROPRIATE TECHNOLOGY

This chapter traces the growth of "Green Technology," the engineering of things and processes to cooperate with the processes of the earth, for the mutual advantage of the earth and its human inhabitants. Its essential message is very simple: If we design our artifacts to appropriate scale, operation, and relation to the world and to their human operators, the natural environment will benefit and so will we.

This move to "appropriate technology" got its start from the seminal work of E. F. Schumacher in *Small Is Beautiful*.[2] Schumacher may have been the first to define "sustainability," as what he called "permanence"— "Nothing makes economic sense unless its continuance for a long time can be projected without running into absurdities."[3] At the outset of the treatise, Schumacher points out that the capital used in the production process is predominantly "provided by nature and not by man—and we do not even recognize it as such."[4] This "natural capital," as he calls it, includes at least fossil fuels, and he points out that we are treating these capital assets as income.

> The liquidation of these capital assets is proceeding so rapidly that even in the allegedly richest country in the world [the U.S.] . . . there are many worried

men, right up to the White House . . . demanding ever more gigantic efforts to search for and exploit the remaining treasures of the earth.[5]

This was in 1973! He pointed out that renewable fuels—wind, small-scale water, solar, and possibly commercially sold wood—accounted for no more than 4 percent of the world's total, and that within the half century, they would be expected to carry 90 percent of the load. Our reckless use of these resources is one major assault on our heritage of capital. (That use is quite literal: "reckless" means "not reckoning," not taking account, both in the sense of failing to consider consequences and in the sense of not bothering to count the cost.) But there is more to the problem:

> Fossil fuels are merely a part of the "natural capital" which we steadfastly insist on treating as expendable, as if it were income, and by no means the most important part. If we squander our fossil fuels, we threaten civilization; but if we squander the capital represented by living nature around us, we threaten life itself.[6]

The major threat that Schumacher saw in the early 1970s, as a second assault on our natural heritage, came from pollution, especially the pollution caused by the manufacture, use, and deposit in the ecosystem of substances such as organochlorines (synthetic fusions of a chlorine atom into organic molecules) not known to nature, exceeding the tolerance margins of nature (margins which themselves may be counted as part of our inherited capital). The third kind of natural capital he saw being recklessly spent as part of "modern industrialism" was the human capital of dignity and satisfaction with life, largely by the reduction of employment to repetitive unskilled motions (when it was not ended altogether). Our problem is an "inability to recognize that the modern industrial system, with all its intellectual sophistication, consumes the very basis on which it has been erected."[7]

The problem, he was not the first (nor the last) to say, lies with our materialism, our pursuit of material goods as both means to the satisfactions of life and as the scorecard of our success in the human enterprise. The world's great religions, like the philosophers, have told us that materialism is unworthy of the unique capacities we have been given, and displeasing to God. Schumacher points out that materialism is not only spiritually unworthy, but incompatible with the natural world.

> An attitude to life which seeks fulfillment in the single-minded pursuit of wealth—in short, materialism—does not fit into this world, because it contains within itself no limiting principle, while the environment in which it is placed is strictly limited.[8]

The point is worth considering. Everything in nature is limited. Nature not only knows when and how to start, it knows when to stop. Trees do not reach the sky; they could not survive if they continued to grow much beyond their present normal height, adjusted over millennia for the other characteristics of their species. Mice do not grow to elephantine size, no matter what you feed them, and most of their systems would surely fail if they grew even to the size of the cats that eat them. Everything in nature (that is not terminated earlier by predation or accident) grows to its mature size, stops, wears itself out in its appointed days, and dies, returning its resources to the earth for reuse.

Ecosystems, too, reach their natural balance at maturity and expand no more. That makes them, in current parlance, "closed systems." Only humans have devised "open systems," systems that can theoretically expand without limit. The systems most famously open, and most troubling in their implications, are Science, the fund of knowledge, and information available to the human species, and the Market, the money system that forms the backbone of our understanding of economics. Science can grow without limits (and has, for the last five centuries at least), and there is no limit to wealth. As long as we can add one to any number you can think of, we can get richer.

But the unlimited increase of wealth, Schumacher argues, is not only contrary to any natural system, it also makes no human sense. Unlimited economic growth runs afoul of common sense on two counts. First, it presupposes unlimited resources, which there are not, and second, it entails terrible interference with natural processes, in the form of global warming, chemical pollution, and nuclear hazard. But worse than that, the unlimited pursuit of wealth distorts human thinking, and misdirects human striving and growth.

> If human vices such as greed and envy are systematically cultivated, the inevitable result is nothing less than a collapse of intelligence. A man driven by greed or envy loses the power of seeing things as they really are, of seeing things in their roundness and wholeness, and his very successes become failures.[9]

They destroy "intelligence, happiness, serenity, and thereby the peacefulness of man."

> The hope that the pursuit of goodness and virtue can be postponed until we have attained universal prosperity and that by the single-minded pursuit of wealth, without bothering our heads about spiritual and moral questions, we could establish peace on earth, is an unrealistic, unscientific and irrational hope.[10]

It is time, he argues, for the sake of our own psychological health, to pursue wisdom, spiritual and moral truth, central to which is permanence, or sustainability. That means that human beings must reduce their perceived "needs" to real needs, beginning with the effort not to cultivate more of them.

Every increase of needs tends to increase one's dependence on outside forces over which one cannot have control, and therefore increases existential fear.[11]

In place of fear we must put wisdom. Science and technology have to "incorporate wisdom into their very structure," wisdom which "demands a new orientation of science and technology toward the organic, the gentle, the non-violent, the elegant and beautiful."[12]

As a beginning application of wisdom, he develops the now-famous notion of appropriate (or intermediate) technology. We need "methods and equipment which are cheap enough so that they are accessible to virtually everyone; suitable for small-scale application; and compatible with man's need for creativity."[13] His argument is the same as that presented by Gandhi, on the effort to rebuild India. "If we feel the need of machines, we certainly will have them. Every machine that helps every individual has a place, but there should be no place for machines that concentrate power in a few hands and turn the masses into mere machine minders, if indeed they do not make them unemployed." He goes on:

> That soul-destroying, meaningless, mechanical, monotonous, moronic work is an insult to human nature which must necessarily and inevitably produce either escapism or aggression, and that no amount of 'bread and circuses' can compensate for the damage done—these are facts which are neither denied nor acknowledged but are met with an unbreakable conspiracy of silence—because to deny them would be too obviously absurd and to acknowledge them would condemn the central preoccupation of modern society as a crime against humanity.[14]

He proceeds with a blanket condemnation of the science of economics, because all its judgments are

> necessarily and *methodically* narrow. For one thing, they give vastly more weight to the short than to the long term. . . . And then, second, they are based on a definition of cost which excludes all 'free goods,' that is to say, the entire God-given environment, except for those parts of it that have been privately appropriated.[15]

As a result of its chosen method, economics systematically ignores the natural world.

Now, who decided all this—that natural capital is to be accounted as income, or ignored altogether, and that the work of a human being is to be counted only as a cost and not as a product? As Schumacher points out, economics operates well only inside a very narrow box of definitions and presuppositions, and this framework of "givens" lies entirely outside of economics. As a result, economics cannot address the major problems of our time, for they all stem from the impact of our industrial civilization on the natural world, the quality of human life, and the future of the race. As a matter of fact, "economics, as currently constituted and practiced, acts as a most effective barrier against the understanding of these problems, owing to its addiction to purely quantitative analysis and its timorous refusal to look into the real nature of things."[16]

How would a Buddhist economist (not that there are such) see the fundamental directions of an economy? Schumacher begins by pointing out that if labor, a person's work for a day, is only "a cost" for the employer and only "a means to the paycheck" for the employee, it loses all worth and content, "the ideal from the point of view of the employer is to have output without employees, and the ideal from the point of view of the employee is to have income without employment."[17] Yes; that sounds like us. The imperative of division of labor (see the pin factory praised in *Wealth of Nations*), all the way to automation and robotization, follows with no further steps. Buddhism sees the matter rather differently. The function of work is (at least)

> To give a man a chance to utilize and develop his faculties; to enable him to overcome his ego-centredness by joining with other people in a common task; and to bring forth the goods and services needed for a becoming existence.[18]

The contrast between the two systems, ours and the Buddhist, is comical: In the Buddhist system, the

> ownership and the consumption of goods is a means to an end, and Buddhist economics is the systematic study of how to attain given ends with the minimum means.
>
> Modern economics, on the other hand, considers consumption to be the sole end and purpose of all economic activity, taking the factors of production— land, labor and capital—as the means. The former, in short, tries to maximize human satisfactions by the optimal pattern of consumption, while the latter tries to maximize consumption by the optimal pattern of productive effort.[19]

Needless to say, it takes a lot less effort to achieve the Buddhist maximization.

The "Buddhist" approach to economics brings us back to the questions that occupied us in the last part of Chapter 1: How ought we to live our lives in order to flourish as human beings? How ought we to live out a personal moral imperative to virtue? Schumacher has already given us a glimpse of a new approach to virtue ethics: Wisdom is the incorporation of sustainability in all our economic thinking; "temperance" re-emerges as control of needs; and a new virtue, simplicity, assumes a central place for human life. Clearly, if you simplify your life in all of its aspects, you will minimize the resources that go into maintaining that life.[20]

In the end, Schumacher's major concern is to distinguish between natural capital—the nonrenewable, irreplaceable, gifts of nature—and the renewable store of goods and services. Perhaps it would help if we learn to think of natural capital—our oceans, forests, wetlands, plains, and the bountiful sea of air that surrounds us—as great works of art. It would not be a neat source of income to sell off all our national collections of art so we could increase our standard of consumption, would it? Can we imagine the French selling off the Cathedral of Notre Dame de Paris for reduction to gravel, or the Greeks selling off the Parthenon for your garden's marble chips? Yet the services that undisturbed natural areas provide for us are worth far more, in sheer survival as well as in beauty, than all the great works of art on the earth.

NATURAL CAPITALISM: ASSESSING THE DAMAGE AND CHANGING THE MINDSET

In some ways, *Natural Capitalism,* the groundbreaking 1999 book by Paul Hawken and Amory and Hunter Lovins of Rocky Mountain Institute,[21] is a refreshing update of Schumacher's work. But a generation primed to accept the triumph of capitalism after 40 years of the Cold War will find the authors' pragmatic cost-conscious approach much more agreeable than Schumacher's communitarianism. They begin the work with what surely reads like a utopian vision of a restored earth, with human houses that produce more energy than they consume, transport that is silent and free from emissions, factories that clean the water they use, and all humans, even the higher number of humans expected in the next century, adequately housed and well fed. But it is no utopia, they insist. The technology to accomplish this is almost complete, and it could be in place in a matter of decades.

> Through this transformation, society will be able to create a vital economy that uses radically less material and energy. This economy can free up resources, reduce taxes on personal income, increase per-capita spending on social ills (while simultaneously reducing those ills), and begin to restore the damaged environment of the earth. These necessary changes done properly can promote economic efficiency, ecological conservation, and social equity.[22]

The rest of the book says how. They begin with a set of facts that should surprise no one.

> In the past half century, the world has lost a fourth of its topsoil and a third of its forest cover. At present rates of destruction, we will lose 70 percent of the world's coral reefs in our lifetime, host to 25 percent of marine life. In the past three decades, one-third of the planet's resources, its 'natural wealth', has been

consumed. We are losing freshwater ecosystems at the rate of 6 percent a year, marine ecosystems by 4 percent a year. There is no longer any serious scientific dispute that the decline in every living system in the world is reaching such levels that an increasing number of them are starting to lose, often at a pace accelerated by the interactions of their decline, their assured ability to sustain the continuity of the life process.[23]

Their criticism is not aimed at the usual villains of industry or bureaucracy, but at the accountants. Who is minding the store? How can the foundation of industry be undermined without something showing up on the balance sheet? Capitalism as we know it, industrial capitalism or financial capitalism, is a "nonsustainable aberration" in the history of human institutions. It fails even to obey its own accounting principles: "It liquidates its capital and calls it income. It neglects to assign any value to the largest stocks of capital it employs—the natural resources and living systems, as well as the social and cultural systems that are the basis of human capital."[24] It notoriously fails to value appropriately the "human capital" upon which it depends—not just the strength of the laborer or the skills of the computer operator, but the solidarity of the community that keeps the worker showing up for work on time in the morning and makes him ashamed to steal from his employer. (The failures of capitalism in the post-Cold War states of the former Soviet Union are instructive; the cultural infrastructure for capitalism was not in place, and the system collapsed in venality.) But most of all it fails to acknowledge, assign value to, and steward appropriately, the natural capital that it inherited.

> *Natural capital* includes all the familiar resources used by humankind: water, minerals, oil, trees, fish, soil, air, et cetera. But it also encompasses living systems, which include grasslands, savannas, wetlands, estuaries, oceans, coral reefs, riparian corridors, tundras, and rainforests. These are deteriorating worldwide at an unprecedented rate."[25]

How could we put a value on the world's resources? It has been estimated that "biological services flowing directly into society from the stock of natural capital are worth at least $36 trillion annually." If that's the income from the endowment, the world's natural capital would have to be valued at between $400 and $500 trillion.[26] The trouble with putting a price tag on the natural resources of the world is that it seems to imply that they are fungible, that other resources of similar price could take their place if we ran out of them. They aren't. There are no oxygen substitutes, for instance. There is no substitute or replacement for the carbon cycle.

The enormous waste of our natural capital is not the fault, as they see it, of the ruthless exploitation of the natural world undertaken by greedy business types aiming only for profit. Instead they indict the deliberate distortions of the marketplace, in the form of policies like subsidies to industries that extract raw materials from the earth and damage the biosphere. As long as it is assumed that there are "free goods" in the world—pure water, clean air, hydrocarbon combustion, virgin forests, veins of minerals—large-scale, energy- and materials-intensive manufacturing methods will dominate.[27]

What the authors suggest is that we take all our capital seriously, and aim for profits that benefit the bottom line for all of the factors. The authors have no objections to capitalism. They just want it done right. Natural capitalism is based on some fundamental assumptions at variance with current capitalistic practices. The environment is not seen as an endless source of free material, but as the condition for all human activity, and the limiting factor in future economic development. The major engines of waste are misconceived, badly designed, or flatly perverse institutions, in business and in government, as well as population growth and wasteful patterns of consumption. In the course of halting the waste, enough extra productivity will be obtained from our resources that we will be able to solve global problems of employment and inequity at the same time. The change will amount to a new industrial revolution, bringing radical changes for the better into our lives. The only form of government compatible with the necessary changes is democracy, but a more complete democracy, one that involves all the people.[28]

The progress they urge—and for the most part confidently foresee—includes a tenfold increase in the efficiency of our use of all resources, the discovery of much less damaging, wasteful, and expensive ways to make our products by imitating the way similar products are made in nature (biomimicry), a changeover from product orientation to service orientation (the products become means, not ends), and a program of reinvestment in the natural systems that we are currently degrading. Not only will these changes preserve the beauty of the world by protecting its natural processes, they are the only condition in which we may avoid the deadly wars over natural resources and make it possible to have peace in the world.

Natural Capitalism joins (and spearheads) a growing literature on the possibilities of organizing capitalism to protect the environment. (The authors gratefully acknowledge the influence, for instance, of James P. Womack and Daniel T. Jones, *Lean Thinking*,[29] born of those writers' work with Taiichi Ohno, 1912–1990, who organized the Toyota Production System.) In the sections that follow we will sketch out just four major areas in which *Natural Capitalism* and other current literature demonstrate that environmentally sound practices would also yield spectacular savings in all other measures as well. In an order suggested by the general level of American interest in things, we will consider the automobile, the family home, the drinking water and the dump.

Green Automobiles

The automobile is generally seen as the chief obstacle to environmental progress, and justifiably so. In the United States alone, it consumes eight million barrels of oil every day (450 gallons per person annually), kills 50,000 people a year in accidents (for a total death toll exceeding that of all the wars in our history), not to mention about a million wild animals a week and tens of thousands of domestic pets, and creates seven billion pounds of unrecycled waste in the course of a year. Its toxic emissions are to blame for one quarter of the "greenhouse gases," the gases that trap the heat of the sun in the atmosphere, bringing about the slow warming of the globe. It pollutes the air in all major urban areas, increasing asthma, emphysema, heart disease, and bronchitis; in some cases, especially in California, the automobile exhaust has made the cities' air unbreathable for parts of the worst days. The roads on which it drives now comprise a paved area equal to all the arable land in the states of Ohio, Indiana, and Pennsylvania, and are maintained at a cost of more than $200 million per day. Its consumption of gasoline costs us $60 billion in foreign oil every year, much of which must be purchased from the politically unstable Persian Gulf area, leaving us prey to extortion from hostile or potentially hostile nations who are not friendly to democracy. Ironically, these purchases are contributing to the area's instability, by funding the war machines of the nations' dictators.[30] Nor is the car any miracle of engineering:

> The contemporary automobile, after a century of engineering, is embarrassingly inefficient: Of the energy in the fuel it consumes, at least 80 percent is lost, mainly in the engine's heat and exhaust, so that at most only 20 percent is actually used to turn the wheels. Of the resulting force, 95 percent moves the car, while only 5 percent moves the driver, in proportion to their respective weights. Five percent of 20 percent is one percent—not a gratifying result from American cars that burn their own weight in gasoline every year.[31]

The situation is getting much worse. As the century opens, Americans want more cars per person—all newer houses in suburban neighborhoods have three bays in the garage. And the cars are getting much larger—the "Sport-Utility Vehicles (SUVs)," built on the model of trucks, compete for a growing market in size and weight, consuming much more gasoline than standard cars, projecting an image of intimidation while compiling a frightening record of rollover deaths.

The SUVs, or "light trucks," deserve special mention and consideration, for they epitomize the problems with the American car (and a few other problems, too). First, they are very dangerous. They are dangerous to their occupants: Their high center of gravity radically increases the risk of rollover if curves are taken at high speeds, while their weight puts an unaccustomed strain on the tires—especially if the tires are underinflated in order to provide more stability on the curves. (This feature of the breed was responsible for the blowup between Ford and Bridgestone-Firestone Tires in 1999-2000.[32]) And they are very dangerous to the occupants of anything they may hit, because they are much heavier than the other cars on the road and their bumpers are placed higher, ensuring a death-dealing invasion of the passenger compartment of a traditional sedan in any high-speed collision. Such collisions are made more likely by the fact that the ordinary householders who buy these trucks are not accustomed or prepared to deal with the height or the weight of the vehicle, and often fail to see obstacles clearly enough, or put on the brakes soon enough or hard enough. Second, the SUV is an unmitigated assault on the natural environment. Its large size and weight require a larger amount of all raw materials to manufacture, without providing services for any more people. Because of its extra weight, the SUV gets abominable gas mileage; it puts a strain on the remaining petroleum supplies on earth, and releases about twice as much carbon dioxide into the atmosphere as an automobile. This change adds significantly to the greenhouse gases: While the average American car puts an alarmingly high 10,168 pounds of carbon dioxide into the air yearly, the SUV dumps a disgraceful 11 *tons* into the atmosphere.[33] Third, to the extent that the SUV is used for its intended purpose, it is an intolerable burden on some of the most fragile ecosystems in the country—the desert, dune, and mountain ecosystems, especially along threatened coastlands and the mountains of the West, that it is supposed to be able to navigate for the pleasure of its owner. Fourth, it usually is not used for that purpose, and to that extent represents a meaningless and unnecessary risk to occupants, others, and the environment, not to mention an unnecessary expense, for it is very expensive. Fifth, its entire appeal which now stands in need of explanation, since it is not used for what it was designed for, so apparently represents a totally unnecessary sacrifice of money for a risky vehicle that does clear and measurable damage to the natural world—rests on a distorted fantasy of masculinity terribly harmful in itself (for a good many reasons), but carefully cultivated and expanded, apparently only to improve the profits picture of a few large corporations. We will return to the fantasy in Chapter 3. For the moment, we need only take note of an American phenomenon that endangers the natural world for absolutely no reason at all. Meanwhile, American habits of consumption are spreading over the rest of the world, especially the developing world, ensuring that any gains in prosperity among those nations will quickly be turned into cars, roads, and as soon as possible, SUVs, to continue the assault against what remains of the natural environment.

Yet it doesn't have to be this way. There are powerful indications that the automotive industry can change. Technology is already available to make the American car safer while putting much less of a demand on environmental resources. We might start with the size, weight, and materials of the automobile. Following in the footsteps of Henry Ford, the automakers use steel, which is strong, attractive, and very heavy. A typical six-seat Ford Taurus, for instance, weights about 3,140 pounds. Using lighter but more expensive materials such as aluminum and magnesium, concept cars have been shown that are much lighter. If the whole–metal body is replaced by molded composite materials, embedding carbon, Kevlar, glass, and other fibers in molded plastics, we can get the weight down to about 1,300 pounds. A smaller sedan might weigh as little as 1000 pounds. The lighter car translates into greater efficiency in several ways: Much less power is needed to accelerate the car, so the engine can be smaller and lighter; because much less power is needed to stop the car, the brakes can be lighter; and with less weight on the tires, they lose less energy in heat.[34] (As the car becomes lighter, some features, like power steering and power brakes, might become completely unnecessary.) Nor is the light car "less safe" than a heavy one, as anyone who has watched the Indianapolis 500 race will appreciate. The race cars are made of ultralight composites, and despite terrible crashes, the race cars' safety systems usually prevent serious injury to the driver.[35] Anything that can keep a driver safe in a crash into the wall at 150 miles per hour should be able to keep driver and passengers safe at road speeds.

If the car can be made substantially more efficient by changing the materials of which it is made, can we continue the efficiencies by improving on the internal combustion engine—possibly getting away from gasoline altogether? We have been talking about electric cars for the entire lifetime of the automobile. Very small cars that travel slowly for short distances before being recharged—golf carts—work very well on battery power alone. But the batteries are too heavy and slow to run a normal car for any range. (Given our present energy resources, a complete changeover to electric cars would not save us any fossil fuels; the batteries must be recharged from the utility grid, and our power plants generally run on fossil fuel. The result of such a changeover would be a net decrease in energy efficiency.) The best way to carry energy is in the form of some compressed fuel, which is changed into electric energy by a small onboard engine as the car moves. Such a system is called "hybrid electric propulsion," and hybrid cars seem to be the wave of the near future. Hybrids could use gasoline or any clean alternative fuel, including biofuel, made from organic waste.[36] Hybrids on the road now (the Toyota Prius, for example) are essentially electric cars that carry a small power plant on board to generate electricity as needed. They work; the car is surely driveable, if heavily subsidized. But the cleanest way to power any car would be from hydrogen fuel cells, which combine hydrogen and oxygen to make energy in a process that has only water as its byproduct. How does the fuel cell work? Peter Fairley presents a brief description in *Technology Today:*

Though fuel cells come in half a dozen varieties, utilizing different fuels and materials, one version has emerged as the clear favorite for automotive use: the proton exchange membrane (PEM) fuel cell. A PEM cell is solid and compact and operates at a relatively cool 80°C. The heart of the PEM cell is a rubbery plastic membrane coated with a platinum catalyst. The catalyst splits hydrogen gas into protons and electrons; only the protons can pass through the membrane. The electrons travel around the membrane, generating the treasured electric current, before recombining with the protons and oxygen on the other side of the membrane to generate water. Stacking a series of these membrane-catalyst assemblies, or "cells," multiplies the voltage.[37]

Where can that hydrogen come from? A prototype just built by DaimlerChrysler uses a sophisticated onboard refinery to generate hydrogen from methanol.[38] Other possibilities include generating the hydrogen from gasoline, which has the advantage of making the transition from the old cars to the new cars a simple one, but the disadvantage of duplicating a chemical manufacturing plant under the hood of the car. For instance, the reactions needed to release hydrogen occur at 800 degrees C, and the chemistry is "temperamental."[39] Nevertheless, GM and Exxon Mobil have announced plans to attempt such a vehicle. DaimlerChrysler is experimenting with methanol. Both methanol and gasoline have the disadvantage of toxicity, including serious threats to human health. The best solution would be to carry around a supply of pure hydrogen. That's how the "hypercars" recommended in Chapter 2 of *Natural Capitalism* avoid these problems. But with contemporary technology, hydrogen is hard to get into a fuel tank (a standard fuel tank conventionally packed with hydrogen would take you no more than 90 miles), and it leaks out easily, causing fires (which are not as dangerous as gasoline fires, but still dangerous). Hydrogen can be liquefied, but then it has to be stored at –253 C, just 20 (Celsius) degrees above absolute zero (40 degrees Fahrenheit). Our cars can't do that. Possibly we could put carbon fibers in the gas tanks, which will absorb more hydrogen in usable form. "Graphite fibers with intricate nanostructures, for example, have been shown to absorb more than 20 percent hydrogen by weight, allowing far more of the gas to be stuffed into a tank."[40]

What is fascinating in this development of the new automobile—the automobile of the future—is that the largest automobile makers are behind it, convinced that the days of the internal combustion engine are limited. Fairley's interviews with the engineers working on this new technology keep returning to Bruce Kopf, director of THINK Technologies, Ford's electric car division. At the end, Ford is enthusiastic about fuel cell technology (despite projections of many years of lower profits), because "[t]he fuel cell promises to make the automobile *sustainable*, cutting pollution and freeing it from the politics of oil—and ensuring that Ford can make as much of a killing in this century as it did in the last."[41] The combination of motivating energies in the statement is remarkable: First, the automakers are engaging in long-term planning, disregarding profits in the present quarter to position their companies for the long haul (since the early 1980s, we have learned not to expect this). Second, they are doing it in order to make money eventually, which reassures us of their sincerity. Third, they are doing it in the recognition that the automobile's relationship with the natural environment—its ability to carry on its work without draining or poisoning natural capital—will decide its future.

Kopf's vision expands: Pure hydrogen does not exist in nature, but must be produced from water b electrolysis. If wind and solar energy could be harnessed to accomplish that separation, "You could make a fuel system and vehicle that produces zero greenhouse gases and zero tailpipe emissions—a hydrogen-oxygen-water cycle that is sustainable forever. That's the ultimate goal."[42]

Of course, creating such a sustainable system would require whole new systems for fueling—can you imagine hydrogen tanks in every service station?

> Graham Batcheler, president of Texaco Energy Systems, the oil giant's advanced-fuels subsidiary in Houston, says the company believes that the fuel cell will replace the internal combustion engine over the long haul. He considers it inevitable that drivers will be filling up with hydrogen—and he wants them to do it at a Texaco station. . . . Texaco is investing in the key technology to make hydrogen fueling possible: advanced storage tanks.[43]

The new technology, the technology that will make automobile travel sustainable, is already with us (in need of tweaking), and while the political will to curb the excesses of the automobile may not be present in our political bodies, we don't need it; private enterprise, for its own profit with us as its customers, is perfectly capable of achieving sustainability on its own.

The problem of the American car stems not only from the SUV syndrome—the taste for larger and heavier and less fuel-efficient cars—but also from the three-bay syndrome—the need for more and more cars, of whatever description. The key to cleaner air is not only better cars, but fewer, driven less. It has been a commonplace of American reform literature for the better part of the 20th century, that we should build excellent public transit systems and somehow have people use them; American political will has never been up to building those systems or to creating the incentives necessary to get them to work. But capitalism has the answer. The only reason that public roads and parking are so inexpensive is that they are heavily subsidized by the government from tax money. Let the public pay the full cost of the roads and parking places they use, and mass transit, of whatever quality, will suddenly become more attractive.[44] The extra income suddenly available to mass transit, provided only that there is real competition among the modes of transit, will make it financially advantageous to improve mass transit services, and the public (now and in the future) will be better served.[45]

Why do we want to own three cars? Well, we want a small car to travel to work or market or station, alone; we want a minivan to carry the soccer team; and we want (depending on taste) an SUV for off-road driving on the weekends, or a truck to carry large loads, or a red convertible to show off for the girlfriend. But then, why would it not be more efficient for a neighborhood to pool resources and own a whole fleet of cars? The only one a single family would need would be a small and fuel-efficient coupe for local use. (More efficient communities would reduce this vehicle to a bicycle; see next sections.) The minivan, roadster, truck, even an SUV, could be owned by all and available on a sign-up basis. We know that this system works:

> Carsharing in Berlin, now spreading across Europe, cuts car ownership by three-fourths and car commuting by nearly 90 percent, yet retains full mobility options.[46]

And a carsharing experiment in the United States is already in place in Portland, Oregon.[47] This is not rocket science. The system makes eminently good sense.

Green Houses

The second great unsustainable in the American landscape, and next target of environmentalist criticism, is generally the American suburban house. The suburbs themselves are targeted for their dependence on the car. But the freestanding house on the large lot in the suburbs is an independent assault on the environment. On the average, the American single-family home emits 16,522.3 pounds of carbon dioxide from its use of electricity generated in plants that burn fossil fuels. If it burns oil in the furnace, it costs 17,622.0 pounds of carbon dioxide to heat the house (natural gas lowers the amount to 11,094.3 pounds).[48] That's about 30,000 lbs, or 15 short tons, per family. And it's getting worse. The house that now sells best on the American market is the "starter castle," or "McMansion," the outsized house with a ballroom-sized two-story front hall, an enormous eat-in kitchen plus breakfast room, formal dining room, family room, perfect for entertaining, with room for the two children, the corgis, and the *au pair*. All this room will require more fuel to light, to heat, and to supply electricity for the entertainment centers, computers, fax machines, and kitchen appliances. Nor does this total include the amount of gasoline burned in mowing the lawn with power mowers, or blowing leaves into a pile with power-driven leaf blowers so that they can be vacuumed into a truck and driven to the dump.

Can something be done about the American home? Brian Lavendel documents the story of a particularly inventive (and responsible) home-owner in the March-April 2001 issue of *Audubon*. Making only those changes available to a suburban homeowner over a period of a few years, the Jonathan Foley family of Wisconsin cut their annual carbon dioxide emissions by two-thirds, to about 15,000 pounds from 42,000 (that included changing the use of the family car). They downsized the house, in the course of moving closer to work and cutting down on the commute. They abolished the lawn, changing to groundcover and raised beds for the garden. Their new house already had two solar panels on the roof to heat their water, and Low-E (low emittance) windows that save heat in the house; at night they pull some panels over them to keep the heat from escaping. And they purchased (one by one) a line of energy-saving appliances, from furnace to refrigerator to dishwasher to washing machine. They try not to use the dryer.

That two-thirds reduction was achieved in a house already built, with household appliances already on the market.[49] What might be done if we could design homes from scratch? It is commonplace that 85 percent of the expenses of maintaining a building are built into the design. The authors of *Natural Capitalism* take on that question, and go beyond it. Beside the materials and construction of the individual house, what can be done about the design of the community itself? One of the experiments that they describe, a subdivision called Village Homes, in Davis, California, serves as a model for "new urbanism," a reintegration of living, working, playing, and neighborliness that the intellectual descendents of Lewis Mumford have urged as an antidote to sprawling growth.[50] (For instance, the residents are allowed to run small businesses out of their homes; a network of pedestrian and bike paths connect all the houses, which are not separated by any roads.) But Village Homes has an environmental twist. It was laid out to maintain the natural drainage of the land, allowing the natural watercourses to form greenways around which the homes are grouped. Narrow roads then interleaf the greenways, situating all cars behind the houses, which face on the greenways. Extensive use is made of trees for natural cooling, and the houses make maximal use of passive solar design, cutting the average household energy bill by one–half to two–thirds. But that was built in the 1970s. With improved materials, we can do much better now.

Since the 1980s we have known how to insulate our houses well, adapting practices from Scandinavia and Canada. For instance, the authors describe their home institution:

> The Rocky Mountain Institute's 4000-square–foot headquarters stands at an elevation of 7,100 feet in western Colorado in a climate that occasionally gets as cold as –47 degrees F. There is only a 52-day nominal growing season between hard frosts here, and midwinter cloudy spells last as long as 39 days. Still the building has no heating system aside from two small woodstoves. Yet

its 99 percent space-heating savings made it cost *less* than normal to build in 1982-84, because its superinsulation, superwindows, and 92 percent efficient heat-recovering ventilators added less cost than was saved up front by eliminating the furnace and ductwork. Moreover, the structure was able to save half the water usage, about 99 percent of the water-heating energy, and 90 percent of the household electricity—for which the bill, if the building were only a house, would be about five dollars a month, before taking credit for its manifold larger photovoltaic power production. The energy savings repaid all the costs of those efficiency improvements in ten months. That was achieved with 1983 technology; today's are better and cheaper.[51]

All that, and it's fun to work in, beautiful to contemplate in its tropical vegetation and turtles, and every year they harvest bananas. Capital costs for building a superinsulated home can be less than for a normal home, because the extra expenditure in caulking the usual leaks and installing the specialized windows is paid back by savings on heating and cooling equipment. The technology also exists to retrofit houses with insulation, to seal leaks in walls and ducts, and to glaze old windows so that they insulate almost as well as the new superwindows. Appliances, as the Foleys discovered, are rapidly increasing in efficiency, and soon levels of energy efficiency may become established by statute. A study by the Technical University of Denmark

> . . . found that combining all the appliance improvements demonstrated by 1989 could save three-fourths of appliances' total electricity while providing the same or better services. The extra cost involved would be recouped in fewer than four years—the equivalent of a bank account paying about 22 percent annual interest tax-free. A decade later, the technologies are even better.[52]

We can build buildings in which the energy requirements are covered almost entirely by gravity and design for passive solar energy. Then, if we put photovoltaic panels on the building, we can produce electricity that the building will not need. At this point the building becomes a power plant—like a tree, it produces more energy than it uses, energy that is now available to us for other purposes. Turning all our buildings into small power plants may be the solution to most of the energy problem of the future.

Sustainable Water

We have known for a long time that a water crisis—an irremediable shortfall in the amount of fresh, drinkable, water available to the world—lies in our immediate future. Climate changes, whether or not brought about at least in part by deforestation and abuse of the land, have created deserts where the "Fertile Crescent" once lay, and spreads them throughout sub-

Saharan Africa; while water is everywhere, very few drops are drinkable (less than 3 percent is fresh, almost all of that is inaccessible, and the rest is increasingly polluted).[53] Despite heroic efforts at creating reservoirs, cities are becoming short on water; water tables are retreating as increasing amounts are pumped for non-sustainable agriculture.[54] In the immediate future, we will see deadly human conflict on the sites of water scarcity—in the Middle East, more conflicts already turn on water than on oil. In the not–distant future, as the human population doubles over the next century, accessible water is expected to increase not at all (although it may be more fully utilized). There will surely not be enough water for us. More dams and construction projects, less and less popular, are not going to increase water without degrading the environment still more. In the end, they will not be able to keep pace with the population. What will we do without water?

Is it possible to use the resources we have more efficiently—so much more efficiently that sufficient water can be guaranteed to the planet into the foreseeable future? We know that we do not need to use the small supply of clean drinking water the way we do. Certain clear inefficiencies leap to mind. We just washed our car, for instance, and watered our flowers with the water from the tap, our drinking water, the same water we use to flush toilets and mix concrete. We can do better than that. But the inefficiencies that are draining our aquifers and sending the global water supply into crisis are on a far larger scale.

In the United States, the major offender is agriculture, and again, the major reason for that is that water abuse is federally subsidized to an extent that makes efficient water use unable to compete.

> Agriculture is responsible for about twice as much of total U.S. water withdrawals as all buildings, industry, and mining combined. It accounted for 81 percent of all 1995 consumptive use. Eighty-eight percent of the nation's 1995 irrigation water went to 17 western states, where the great majority of all water districts were mining groundwater faster than it was being recharged. This is a long-standing pattern. Freshwater flows from rivers are provided to agriculture under a program of federal subsidies that go back to the nineteenth century. California has built a vast agribusiness sector on water so heavily subsidized that 57 percent of its agricultural water grows four crops that produce only 17 percent of its agricultural revenue. Arizona has long used subsidized water to flood-irrigate cotton and alfalfa in a desert. The states along the Colorado River, including five of the ten fastest-growing states in the United States, have already allocated on paper more water than is actually in the river, and in many years, the river never reaches the sea.[55]

The most notorious waste in the United States is the depletion of the Ogallala Aquifer, which lies under the Great Plains from (at one time) Texas to North Dakota. This is fossil water, trapped underground in the Pleistocene era. Rainwater recharges it to some extent, possibly half an inch per year. But it is being mined at the rate of three to ten feet a year, to grow grain, mostly to fatten cattle for the table. It is difficult to put the tremendous waste involved in this practice into human perspective, but the authors try:

> . . . half to two-thirds of the economically recoverable Texas portion [of the aquifer] was already drained by 1980. Nevertheless, two-fifths of America's feedlot cattle were being fed grain made of Ogallala groundwater. Growing enough of that grain to add sufficient weight on a feedlot steer to put an extra pound of beef on the table consumed up to a hundred pounds of lost, eroded topsoil and over eight thousand pounds of Ice Age-vintage groundwater.[56]

Meanwhile, none of this is necessary. Wherever simple conservation techniques have been tried (such as watering crops only when the soil is dry, instead of all the time), water consumption has been significantly reduced. Whenever truly sustainable irrigation techniques have been put in place— such as placing small amounts of water at the roots of the plants through buried plastic tubes rather than launching large amounts of water through the air in the general direction of the plants through center-pivot irrigation sprinklers—the gains are dramatic. Use of water in one case measurably increased from under half of the amount supplied (the rest lost by evaporation) to 95 percent, and the crop yields improved.[57]

Landscaping creates some of the most wasteful water practices in the developed world. The United States has desert habitat in several states— California, Nevada, Arizona, New Mexico—and near–desert in several bordering states. Yet an admiring article in *TIME* magazine (July 2001) describes a waterfront community, Shadow Lake, under construction in Indio, California. The developer began by buying 96 acres of desert land near Indio, and at the cost of $10 million, covered 46 of them with a lake lined with vinyl. That was expensive, but he expects to make it all back: the "lakefront" lots are selling for $400,000 and up. Marveling at his success, "other developers are rushing to assemble their own desert-lake parcels."[58] And where does this water come from? The Colorado River, through aqueducts and canals already constructed at public expense to supply the City of Los Angeles and the farmers in the Imperial Valley. Some environmentalists and farmers are upset, calling the lake a "poster child for water waste," but California law permits use of the Colorado River water for recreational use, so they have no legal recourse. Supporters of the lake point out that the development, when complete, could add more than $1 million in property taxes, benefiting the community.

Besides, supporters point out, the 12-foot–deep lake loses less water to evaporation than a lawn, since the lawn loses water through all the blades of all the grass, presenting more surface to the air. This is probably true, but not really a defense of the entire project, since all the houses are expected to have lawns, just as all the new housing developments have around Las Vegas, Nevada. The article ends in the 106 ° heat of a desert afternoon, with Shadow

Lake's sprinklers showering the barren hillsides with Colorado River water in order to turn them green for the customers.[59]

Why did we ever end up with lawns in the desert? Developers of the gated communities near desert cities wanted to appeal to retirees from the East, from the Midwest, and from Northern California, especially those suffering from respiratory problems that could be helped by dry air. The developers suspected that their customers wanted to come to the desert for the air, but once there, would select the community that looked the most like home. Hence swimming pools and lawns, all from the water of the Colorado River. Sprinklers have to run 24 hours a day in many of these places, just to keep up with the high evaporation rate of acres of bluegrass, which evolved in rainy Kentucky.

There lies the solution, of course. "The simplest way to eliminate the need for watering landscapes is to replant them with flora that evolution actually fitted to grow there."[60] Desert landscapes are very beautiful, appreciated on their own terms. For the plains, for that matter, prairie grasses are better adapted for life over the Ogallala Aquifer than Kentucky grasses. They absorb what rain they receive better than the shallow-rooted bluegrass, they hold the soil, and they need virtually no watering, thereby saving money as well as our most precious resource.[61]

In the conservation of water as well, two fundamental truths underlie the solutions to the problem. The first is that there is no substitute for good design. We can devise systems to dispose of human waste that do not require the use of large amounts of water; we should do that, rather than tinkering with the present water-borne sanitation system which can never meet the needs of the world.[62] We have designed better irrigation systems; we should use them. We are working now to design manufacturing systems that will recycle the water used in them completely, into a closed loop, to reduce their claims on the local water systems to nothing.[63] The second truth, which explains the present dysfunction of the system and also its resistance to change to the more efficient models, is that government subsidy distorts all rational efforts to improve anything, and should be abolished. Federal subsidies of current patterns of water use, locked in by political influence, stand square in the middle of all reform efforts. On the one hand, new methods represent a threat to the current structure of political power that protects the old ones, so invite political opposition; on the other, with all the water we want so inexpensive, why change anything? If it ain't broke, don't fix it. But of course, it is very badly broke, as this century now upon us will demonstrate.

Green Waste

We have always known (and are probably tired of being told) that we are a wasteful throwaway society, that we generate far too much waste. Tiresome as may be the thought, the numbers are fascinating. The recently closed Fresh Kills Landfill, on Staten Island, New York, used to receive all the trash for New York City's five counties, amounting to

> 26 million pounds of commercial and household waste per day. Covering four square miles and rising more than a hundred feet high, it contain[ed] 2.9 billion cubic feet of trash, consisting of 100 million tons of newspaper, paint cans, potato peels, polystyrene clamshells, chicken bones, soggy breakfast cereals, cigarette butts, Coke cans, dryer lint, and an occasional corpse.[64]

And that's only .018 percent of what we throw out every day; 5500 times that much solid waste ends in other landfills or incinerators elsewhere in the country. The description is doubly persuasive, as a sobering glimpse of the vast problem of the waste itself, and an equally sobering glimpse of our wasteful way of life. Most of that mess shouldn't be there at all: The organics are compostable, the newspaper is recyclable, the Coke cans are at least recyclable and probably returnable, the paint cans are probably toxic and should be disposed of elsewhere, the corpse should be given a funeral and a decent burial, and what are we doing eating junk food, smoking cigarettes, and wasting electricity with a dryer? Viewed from another angle, Americans are responsible for about one million pounds of waste per person per year, including 3.3 trillion pounds of carbon in carbon dioxide gas placed in the atmosphere, 3.5 billion pounds of carpet dumped in landfills, 3.7 trillion pounds of construction debris, and a terrifying 710 billion pounds of hazardous waste generated by chemical production.[65] Total annual wastes are greater than 50 trillion pounds per year; if we count wastewater, water in such bad shape that it cannot be rejoined to the water supply, total waste becomes 250 trillion pounds.[66] Not counted are the estimated millions of pounds of wastes generated by extraction enterprises in the developing world for export to the United States. Incidentally, since Fresh Kills was closed, much of the New York area trash has been loaded onto trucks every morning and brought to Virginia where there are still open landfills. Has anyone measured the fossil fuel involved in such an operation?

In the tally of global waste, we should count the unemployed and the underemployed. The employment picture impacts the natural environment in two very different ways. First, the unemployed or underemployed have to supplement their income. By definition, they cannot do it legally (else they'd be employed). So they do it illegally. How do we deal with crime? We've gone back and forth in this country's history, from "lock-'em-up and throw-away-the-key," to "give them therapy, rehabilitation, and job training." Right now we're back again, to locking up.

> The United States has quietly become the world's largest penal colony. (China ranks second—most Americans have probably bought or used something made in a Chinese prison.) Nearly 5 million men in the United States are awaiting

trial, in prison, on probation, or on parole. In 1997 alone, the number of inmates in county and city jails increased by 9 percent. One out of every twenty-five men in America is involved with the penal or legal system in some way. Nearly one of every three black men in his twenties is in the correctional system.[67]

And that is a terrible waste. It is a waste of land, bricks and mortar, steel, fabrics, energy for heat and light, food and water, landfill space for the trash, and most terribly of people. Not only are the inmates "wasted," lost, all the investment put into them down the drain, but the lives of the people who watch and guard and administer them, while necessarily dedicated to the task, are also lost to production. Somehow there must be some way to rescue this resource.

Second, one of the reasons that there are unemployed is that production processes have become so much more "efficient," in that sense of efficiency that only an industrial capitalism could love. An increase in "efficiency," on the understanding of industrial capitalism, means an increase in worker "productivity," that is, the value of goods turned out by a single worker in a single unit of time (say, one workday). Making workers more productive is not, save marginally, a matter of stronger incentives. In order to make a worker significantly more productive, we extend the length and strength of his arms, first by putting in heavy machinery so that one man may do the work of ten, eventually by putting in computers wired to robotized factories, so that one man may do the work of a thousand. (What happened to the 999? In an industrial or post-industrial economy in the throes of astronomical growth, possibly they all got factories of their own to run. In the real world, some will retire, some will end in jail [or die in hospitals of alcohol–related illnesses], some will get lucky and find a new job with a future, and most will end up in the "service" sector, in marginal jobs.) The "productivity" story, then, is one of substituting machines, manufactured capital, for human capital. Because manufactured capital is always extracted from natural capital, that amounts to substituting natural capital for human capital. That substitution is irrational—literally, counterproductive—at a point in our history when we are running out of natural capital and have human capital to spare (or waste). The waste story is completed with the fact that all of this irrationality is accomplished at far too high a cost in money. It is notorious that it costs as much to keep a man in prison as it does to keep a son at Yale. The effect of the despair and stress caused by unemployment is a national health bill that boggles the mind, much of it for administrative expenses, much more of it devoted to coping with the health effects of lifestyles of waste: heart disease, obesity, pollution-caused lung disease, and substance abuse. The combined result of this wrongheaded notion of "productivity," using much too much of nature to make fewer and fewer people accomplish more work, is that we have created three crises at once:

We are draining our natural capital; we are wasting our human capital; and we are paying for it all with our tax money. Isn't there a better way to live on the earth?

Green Consumption

Suppose we simply change orientations, and think of service, not of product.

First, the reason we are draining natural capital is that we think we need the products of transformation of natural resources (the land now occupied by wetlands to drain for suburban expansion, the iron and steel for the machines, the wood for the houses, the oil for burning) to extend the productivity and the options for living for the human population. But suppose we ask, what are these natural resources worth if we leave them in place? We will obtain an indefinitely (not infinitely) large value for the undisturbed prairie, the uncut forest, the marsh hunting grounds for the duck, if we will but extend our view forward to a time when a much larger population will relish the recreational access to what remains of woods and brooks. But for the moment, there is a value in the trillions of dollars, not for recreational access, but for biological services, of the natural ecosystems of the world. Have we considered that the ecosystems regulate the climate, make the soil fertile, pollinate all our crops so that they give us food, hold the hillsides so they do not become mudslides, control pests, and purify our air and water?[68] In their spare time, the ecosystems of the world produce the oxygen without which we die in minutes. Remember Biosphere II? Acres were given over to an enclosed bubble in which all manner of plants and animals grew and in which eight (8) (no more) humans were to live for a few years. They were out of there in months, sporting oxygen tanks and crawling with cockroaches. We do not know how to duplicate nature's services. We are foolish even to try. Before we continue with our wasteful practices, maybe we should stop to think about the services given us for free; perhaps we should acknowledge their value in monetary terms.

The next reconception of the economy is in the realm of manufactured capital. Let us think not of the material thing that we buy, but of what we want it for, the service that it provides for us. "Any improvement that provides the same or a better stream of *services* from a smaller flow of *stuff*, can produce the same material wealth with less effort, transportation, waste, and cost."[69] Again, the major improvements will be in the design of the system. Chemical engineers have managed, by progressive redesign, to cut in half the amount of energy needed to fabricate their products; they can do better. Systems studies have suggested small design changes (changing the position of a louver in a laboratory fume hood, for instance) that result in 60–80 percent savings in mechanical power. Superinsulation of the furnaces could save a lot of the heat wasted by the glass industry. Tremendous savings can be realized by introducing sensors that regulate heat much more precisely. Fuel cells are more efficient than the most efficient of power generators. There is an enormous potential for savings at every step of every process in every manufacturing enterprise, and "[I]nnovation seems in no danger of drying up."[70] On the principle of biomimicry, we can learn from nature. As the sluggard is to go to the ant for instruction, so the chemical engineer should go to the spider:

> The only thing we have that comes close to [spider] silk . . .is polyaramid Kevlar, a fiber so tough it can stop bullets. But to make Kevlar, we pour petroleum-derived molecules into a pressurized vat of concentrated sulfuric acid and boil it at several hundred degrees Fahrenheit in order to force it into a liquid crystal form. We then subject it to high pressures to force the fibers into alignment as we draw them out. The energy input is extreme and the toxic byproducts are odious. . . . The spider manages to make an equally strong and much tougher fiber at body temperature, without high pressures, heat, or corrosive acids. . . . If we could learn to do what the spider does, we could take a soluble raw material that is infinitely renewable and make a superstrong water-insoluble fiber with negligible energy inputs and no toxic outputs.[71]

She does it all, be it noted, from the materials in chewed–up flies and crickets. It has occurred to some to study this technology; Christopher Viney of Scotland is exploring the silk manufacture of the golden orb-weaver spider to see how such methods might be transferred to human manufacturing. But the transfer has not happened yet, and the funding for such research is meager.[72]

But beyond the efficiency that is still to be realized in the making of things, there is the possibility that we might get precisely the same enjoyment of things without the things being owned. If that sounds strange, consider the landfills: They are piled high, sometimes miles high, with things that once were bought or needed for human enjoyment but are no longer enjoyed, things that have no more use (consider the daily newspaper). If we wish to reduce the landfills, we should make sure that people have something to do with things that they enjoyed but no longer enjoy. Let us once more let nature be our guide. "In nature, nothing edible accumulates; all materials flow in loops that turn waste into food."[73] Can we turn waste into food? William McDonough, former Dean of the University Virginia School of Architecture and one of the pioneers of the new industrial revolution, recounts the development of an upholstery fabric composed of only those chemicals that are free from metals, mutagens, endocrine disruptors, carcinogens, and all other pollutants—a "fabric so safe one could literally eat it." It took a long time in development, but when they had the process down, it started to save money, money that had had to be spent before on disposal of toxic wastes and administration of regulatory compliance.[74] Good design, especially good design that uses the new "nanotechnologies," will ensure that every product is designed from the molecular level onward to fit a specific purpose; nothing unnecessary will come into existence. The same technologies can be used to disassemble products no longer needed.

How many of each thing do we need? Only enough, the authors of *Natural Capitalism* point out, for one to be available whenever someone wants to use it. Some objects we buy not just for use but for beauty (dishes for the table, for instance). If these are made beautiful and durable, there will be no need to change or dispose of them, possibly for generations. All the cost of replacing disposable or fragile non-repairable items will be saved. On the other hand, there are objects that we buy only for use. We do not buy washing machines or lawnmowers just for the joy of looking at them. We buy them to use, and the hours they stand idle are wasted hours, hours when matter, natural capital, has been frozen in place and is doing no work. Such hours should be avoided; the way to avoid them is to make just enough to use, and allot the use in some convenient manner. One obvious way to save materials, for example, is to use community Laundromats instead of forcing individual households to buy their own machines. (It's a good way to get to know your neighbors, too.) Lawnmowers, too, can make the rounds of the neighborhood (for those still sufficiently unenlightened to have lawns). In Portland, Oregon, groups of neighbors have joined an association called Car-Sharing Portland (CSP), which owns a fleet of cars parked on the street in the neighborhood. All members own keys to the fleet, which is maintained by their annual dues and mileage costs. The allotment of cars is achieved the way towns allot their tennis courts: An automated phone system takes the reservation, and they keep track of their mileage with logs. There are similar groups in other cities. Where the group is large enough, the fleet can maintain a large variety of vehicles, from pickup trucks to roadsters, giving its members access to many types of vehicles they could never own.[75]

And what of the inevitable residue, the computers that we use all the time but must be replaced by newer models with ever-increasing frequency, or the family (or fleet) car that has finally worn out and needs replacement, or the packaging that came with the refrigerator, or computer, most of it Styrofoam, that no one needs any more? Take them back to the manufacturer, some European countries have suggested.[76] As a result of "takeback" legislation, packaging recycling went from 12 percent in 1992 to 86 percent in 1997 in Germany, with equally dramatic increases in plastic recycling. In the Netherlands, a 1999 law requires that all computers and a variety of other appliances and equipment be taken back by their manufacturers. Italy is preparing to extend its refrigerator takeback law to other appliances.[77] Over much of Europe, there is a general expectation that packaging, electronics, and batteries will be taken back and recycled. Some manufacturers were ahead of the curve: by 1997, IBM was recovering 35 million pounds of computers and computer parts per year.[78] The idea is catching on. In Minnesota, in October of 2000, Sony Electronics announced (or allowed Governor Jesse Ventura to announce) that for the next five years, the company will fund a program to take back for recycling "any and all outdated Sony products currently in the hands of state consumers."[79]

The goal is zero waste, especially toxic waste. Right now discarded CRTs—cathode ray tubes, as found in TVs and computer monitors—are the largest source of lead in the waste stream. Printed circuit boards are the second largest source. The Sony initiative gets at least its contribution out of the waste stream for good.

> Sony's program, which will spread to five other states in 2001, is the first of its kind in the United States. But such examples of Extended Producer Responsibility (EPR) are business-as-usual throughout Europe, where the concept of legislatively mandating manufacturers to take responsibility for the waste they create has taken firm root.[80]

This initiative is much more demanding on manufacturers, and much more effective, if it works, on removing waste from the landfill than the "recycling" initiatives we have all worked so hard to carry out. As an alternative, it might be asked, why not simply enact more incentives for "extended *product* responsibility," as recommended by Clinton's Council on Sustainable Development in 1996? (On this concept, we as a society acknowledge responsibility—we're not done with anything we own until we have disposed of it in the proper way, with a preference for reusing and recycling—with that responsibility shared among producer, government, and consumer.) The answer is depressing: it doesn't work. When the responsibility is not pinpointed, the product falls through the cracks into the landfill. We don't begin to recycle all we could, and we're doing less each year. The recycling of plastic bottles, for instance, dropped from 53 percent in 1994, which is not exactly outstanding, to a mediocre 35.6 percent in 1998. Why that is, we will cover in the next chapter. Why companies are interested in EPR is much simpler: It gives them valuable information (since the weak points of a product line are best discovered by finding out how they broke down), and it saves material and therefore money. Avoiding the costs of all new material is simply good business.

There are obstacles to overcome in achieving zero waste. A large part of the problem is persuading manufacturers of disposable objects—paper goods, cans, and bottles, for instance—to use recycled material in the manufacturing process. At present, it is easy for the companies to demonstrate that it is often not economically feasible to incorporate recycled materials: after all, there are 15 tax-and-spend subsidies that directly benefit three industries—forestry, petroleum, and mining—whose products directly compete with recycled material. "It doesn't take a rocket scientist to realize that public subsidies for virgin materials puts recycling at a competitive disadvantage," comments Bill Sheehan, national coordinator of the GrassRoots Recycling Network, an activist organization pushing for zero waste.[81]

In the end, the drive for zero waste is more than prudent municipal economics, an aesthetic imperative, or just good business. It is a moral imperative derived from nature itself. As the authors of *Natural Capitalism* put it,

> . . . imagine an industrial system that has no provision for landfills, outfalls, or smokestacks. If a company knew that nothing that came into its factory could be thrown away, and that everything it produced would eventually return, how would it design its components and products? The question is more than a theoretical construct, because the earth works under precisely these strictures.[82]

AN APPRECIATION OF THE POTENTIAL

The conclusion of this very brief exploration is that sustainable living is entirely possible, with technology already in place or likely in the near future. For an extended argument to this effect, we can do no better than recommend a reading of *Natural Capitalism* and a survey of the continuing work of Rocky Mountain Institute and the dozens of other organizations dedicated to an environmentally sustainable future. There are exemplary institutions in place, at the microlevel (the RMI headquarters growing tropical fruit with no furnace) and the macrolevel (the city of Curitiba, Brazil, whose enormous accomplishments in creating and preserving quality of life in conditions of developing nation poverty were observed by Bill McKibben and documented in Chapter 14 of *Natural Capitalism*). If a thing exists, the logicians tell us, then it is possible that it exists. These things have been done, and humans have done them. Therefore we can, too. (That last may not be the case; the question will occupy our attention in the first part of the next chapter.)

Meanwhile we know more. Environmental preaching in the absence of environmental knowledge may be true—use less heat, less water, less gasoline, less heavy machinery, all of which is surely true—but it is not as dramatic and persuasive as detailed knowledge of the green and growing things that are being defended. We are acquiring knowledge of how nature works at unprecedented speed, from the awareness of the value of nature's services to the way humans have interacted usefully with nature for the 50,000 years of human existence prior to the Industrial Revolution. It turns out that the foraging (hunting-gathering) and slash–and–burn farming that preceded the Neolithic agricultural village were not so irrational after all; it turns out that humans have worked out a variety of ways of living in harmony with nature, many of which are still applicable now.[83]

The most fascinating aspects of the new industrial revolution—or the new capitalism, or the new environmentalism, whatever we choose to call it—are the allies signing up for the campaign. "Is it progress if a cannibal uses a fork?" asked the Polish poet Stanislaw Lec. John Elkington, of London's "SustainAbility," a consulting firm for businesses concerned with environmental matters, cheerfully concludes that indeed it is. *Cannibals With Forks* is a blueprint for achieving a positive balance on "the triple bottom line": the requirement for financial profitability, ethical acceptability, and environmental sustainability.[84] He makes no pretense of challenging capitalism. His organization recognizes that the "bottom line" of business will very soon require environmental responsibility, and so it consults on the methods that businesses may take to achieve that new requirement. It is all very matter of fact, and very inevitable.

There are other signs of a growing consciousness of the possibility. As Texaco is planning hydrogen fill-ups for the new generation of fuel cell cars, so Shell is advertising its use of solar energy. Meanwhile major corporations are arranging to cut back their carbon emissions, as wasteful and costly in the long run. Beginning with trading emissions allowances, major oil companies expect to cut emissions by 10 percent by 2002 (Shell) or 2010 (BP).[85] In some isolated cases, multinational corporations (MNCs) have settled into dialogue with the NGOs that opposed their environmental practices, and have actually reached agreements. Even the popular media are beginning to consider the possibilities of sustainable energy use; consider the article, "Personally Empowered," in the *New York Times* of February 25, 2001, in which we find out how to achieve independence from the municipal power supply.[86] All of this is possible, and could be very close. Even from the term, "biomimicry," it seems that we are really learning, as Aldo Leopold put it, to Think Like a Mountain.[87] We have a direction for the future of life on this earth, and its unifying principle, as a practical blueprint for changing the world, is the Land Ethic itself. Be excited. Be very excited.

NOTES

[1] I would much rather read books than write them; I wrote this one only becuse I could not find any other that said what needed to be said about the discovery of a personal ethic in harmony with the land ethic. But I had no intention of inventing wheels that I didn't have to, and gratefully used any that I could find rolling through the literature. In this chapter I am particularly grateful for permission to use, in letter and in spirit, *Natural Capitalism*, by Amory and Hunter Lovins and Paul Hawken of Rocky Mountain Institute. It says everything I want to say about the technology of the sustainable life, backed up by extensive scholarship and practice, and with minor supplementation (like the short discussion of E. F. Schumacher's work in the first section), forms the argument of this chapter.

[2] E. F. Schumacher, *Small Is Beautiful: Economics As If People Mattered*, Introduction by Theodore Roszak, New York: Harper and Row, 1973.

[3]Ibid., pp. 30–31.

[4]Ibid., p. 14.

[5]Ibid., p. 15.

[6]Ibid., p. 16.

[7]Ibid., p. 19.

[8]Ibid., p. 21.

[9]Ibid., p. 29.

[10]Ibid., p. 30.

[11]Ibid., p. 31.

[12]Ibid.

[13]Ibid., pp. 31–32.

[14]Ibid., pp. 35.

[15]Ibid., pp. 41.

[16]Ibid., pp. 45.

[17]Ibid., pp. 51.

[18]Ibid.

[19]Ibid.

[20]Ibid., p. 55.

[21]Paul Hawken, Amory Lovins, and L. Hunter Lovins, *Natural Capitalism: Creating the Next Industrial Revolution*, Boston: Little, Brown & Company, 1999.

[22]Ibid., p. 2.

[23]Ibid., p. 4, citing the Coral Reef Alliance's 1998 report, "Reefs in Danger: Threats to Coral Reefs Around the World," and the 1998 report of the Worldwide Fund for Nature (Europe).

[24]Ibid., p. 5.

[25]Ibid., p. 2.

[26]Ibid., p. 5, citing Robert Costanza et al., "The Value of the World's Ecosystem Services and Natural Capital," *Nature* 387:253–260, May 15, 1997. (Costanza used 1994 dollars in that 1997 report, and came out with $33 trillion in annual ecosystem services.) Also the World Bank's reports of 1995 (*Monitoring Environmental Progress: A Report on a Work in Progress*) and 1997 (*Expanding the Measure of Wealth: Indicators of Environmentally Sustainable Development*), Environmentally Sustainable Development (Studies and Monographs) World Bank, Washington, D.C.

[27]Ibid., p. 15, citing W. R. Stahel and G. Reday-Mulvey, *Jobs for Tomorrow: The Potential for Substituting Manpower for Energy*, New York: Vantage Press, 1981.

[28]Ibid., pp. 9–10, citing William McDonough and M. Braungart, "The Next Industrial Revolution," *Atlantic Monthly* 282 (4): October 1998.

[29]D. T. Jones and J. P. Womack, *Lean Thinking: Banish Waste and Create Wealth in Your Corporation*, New York: Simon & Schuster 1996. This book is summarized by the authors in "Beyond Toyota: How to Root Out Waste and Pursue Perfection," *Harvard Business Review*, September-October 1996, pp. 140–158.

[30]Figures from *Natural Capitalism*, pp. 22–23.

[31]Ibid., p. 24.

[32]See (among other accounts) Keith Bradsher, "Ford Is Conceding S.U.V. Drawbacks . . . but won't stop production," *The New York Times*, May 12, 2000, pp. A1, C2. Or by the same author, "Ford says Firestone Was Aware of Flaw In Its Tires by 1997," *The New York Tiimes*, August 14, 2000, pp. A1, A13. Also Lisa Newton, "How Can We Trust Our Cars Are Safe?" *Newsday*, September 3, 2000.

[33]Brian Lavendel, "GreenHouse," *Audubon*, March-April 2001, p. 78, for figures for automobile; figures for SUV from Keith Bradsher, "How Many Miles Per Gallon? It's Easy: Add Safety, Mileage, Pollution. Divide by Dollars," *The New York Times*, July 29, 2001, Week In Review, p. 3.

[34]*Natural Capitalism*, pp. 27–29.

[35]Ibid., p. 30.

[36]Ibid., pp. 32–33.

[37]Peter Fairley, "Fill 'er Up with Hydrogen," *Technology Today*, November-December 2000, p. 56.

[38]Ibid., pp. 54.

[39]Ibid., p. 58.

[40]Ibid., p. 60.

[41]Ibid., p. 62, emphasis supplied.

[42]Ibid., p. 60.

[43]Ibid., p. 60.

[44]We may be on the way there, at least as far as the parking places are concerned. If you want to park your car in the basement of the North Shore Towers co-op in Floral Park, Queens, you will have to buy a space for $10,000 and then pay common charges. And that's in Queens. In Brooklyn, prices range around $25,000; in Manhattan, prices go from $30,000 up to $80,000. On top of the purchase price, monthly common charges run from $75 to $150. Of course, if you just want to rent a space, you can park in a rental parking garage for only $1000 per month.

[45]Hawken, Lovins, and Lovins, *Natural Capitalism*, pp. 41–43.

[46]Ibid., p. 44, citing E. U. von Wiezsacker, A. B. Lovins, and L. H. Lovins, *Factor Four: Doubling Wealth, Halving Resource Use*, Earthscan, London, available in U.S. through Rocky Mountain Institute.

[47]Brian Lavendel, "GreenHouse," *Audubon*, March-April 2001, p. 78.

[48]Ibid., p. 78.

[49]Incidentally, that article has a sidebar on p. 77 that lists energy-efficient appliances and the 800 numbers to call to reach a convenient outlet; it further lists several websites where more information on energy efficiency in the home can be obtained (including the Energy Star program, the Consortium for Energy Efficiency, and Rocky Mountain Institute, sponsor of *Natural Capitalism*.).

[50]See Peter Calthorpe and William Fulton, *The Regional City: Planning for the End of Sprawl*, Washington DC: Island Press, 2000.

[51]*Natural Capitalism*, p. 102, citing Amory Lovins, *Rocky Mountain Institute Visitor's Guide*, Rocky Mountain Institute Publication, #H-1, Snowmass, CO 1991.

[52]*Natural Capitalism*, p. 106, citing J. S. Norgard, "Low Electricity Appliances—Options for the Future," in T. B. Johansson, *et al.*, *Electricity*, Lund, Sweden: University of Lund Press, 1989.

[53]*Natural Capitalism*, p. 213, citing the United Nations Commission on Sustainable Development report for 1997 and a series of terrifying reports on water pollution generally (note 2). For instance, in China, four-fifths of the rivers are too polluted to sustain fish.

[54]Ibid.

[55]Ibid., p. 215, citing P. H. Gleick *et al.*, *California Water 2020: A Sustainable Vision*, Oakland CA: Pacific Institute for Studies in Development, Environment, and Security, 1995.

[56]Ibid., p. 215, citing J. Bredehoeft, "Physical Limitations of Water Resources," in E. A. Engelbert and A. F. Scheuring, eds., *Water Scarcity: Impacts on Western Agriculture*, Berkeley, CA: University of CA Press, 1984, pp. 17–44.

[57]Ibid., p. 218.

[58]Dan Cray, "Water War: A real estate developer's scheme to build a lake in a desert region seemed ludicrous. But maybe he's not all wet," *TIME*, July 30, 2001, "Bonus" section on Your Business, Y11.

[59]Ibid.

[60]*Natural Capitalism*, p. 219.

[61]Ibid.

[62]Ibid., pp. 220–224.

[63]Ibid., p. 225.

[64]*Natural Capitalism*, p. 51, citing B. Weber, "At the Dump, Wish You Were Here," *New York Times*, March 27, 1996, and W. Rathje and C. Murphy, *Rubbish! The Archeology of Garbage*, New York: HarperCollins, 1992, pp. 3–9.

[65]Ibid., p. 52. The figures on toxic waste are attributed to the Chemical Manufacturers Association (now the American Chemistry Council) in 1993.

[66]Ibid., citing USGS 1995.

[67]Ibid., p. 54, citing P. Mergenhagen, "The Prison Population Bomb," *American Demographics*, February 1996; *San Francisco Chronicle*, "Number of Americans in jail rises again," February 19, 1998, *Criminal Justice Newsletter* "30 percent of Young Black Men Are In Correctional System, Study Finds," 26:19, October 20, 1995.

[68]See Gretchen C. Daily, *Nature's Services: Societal Dependence on Natural Ecosystems*, Washington: Island Press, 1997.

[69]*Natural Capitalism*, p. 62.

[70]Ibid., pp. 64–68.

[71]Ibid., p. 70, citing Janine Benyus, in L. Mishel, *The State of Working America 1996–1997* New York: M. E. Sharpe, 1997.

[72]Janine M. Benyus explores this among other biomimetic research in her 1997 book *Biomimicry: Innovation Inspired by Nature*, The story of Viney's lab was adapted in "Along Came a Spider: why tinker with nature when you can copy it?" in *Sierra*, July/August 2001, pp. 46–47.

[73]Lavendal, "Green House," p. 71.

[74]Ibid., p. 72.

[75]See Lavendel, p. 76.

[76]*Natural Capitalism*, p. 79.

[77]Jim Motavalli, "Zero Waste," *E: The Environmental Magazine*, March/April 2001, pp. 26–33.

[78]*Natural Capitalism*, p. 78, citing the Interagency Workgroup on Industrial Ecology, Material and Energy Flows, *Materials*, final report, January 1998. (White House Council on Environmental Quality et al.).

[79]Motavalli, "Zero Waste."

[80]Ibid., p. 28.

[81]Ibid., pp. 28–29.

[82]*Natural Capitalism*, p. 18.

[83]Evan Eisenberg, *The Ecology of Eden*, New York: Alfred Knopf, 1998.

[84]John Elkington, *Cannibals With Forks: The Triple Bottom Line of 21st Century Business*, Gabriola Island, BC: New Society Publishers, 1998 (first published Oxford, 1997).

[85]Eric Roston, "Warming Up To Green," *TIME*, March Business Section, p. B9, March 19, 2001.

[86]Tom Zeller, "Personally Empowered," *New York Times*, February 25, 2001, p. WK 16.

[87]Aldo Leopold, *A Sand County Almanac, and Sketches from Here and There, New York Times*, New York: Oxford, 1946.

BIBLIOGRAPHY

Benyus, Janine M., *Biomimicry: Innovation Inspired by Nature*. 1997. Excerpted in "Along Came a Spider: Why tinker with nature when you can copy it?"*Sierra*, July/August 2001, pp. 46-47.

Bradsher, Keith, "How Many Miles Per Gallon? It's Easy: Add Safety, Mileage, Pollution. Divide by Dollars," *The New York Times*, July 29, 2001, Week In Review, p. 3.

Bredehoeft, J. "Physical Limitations of Water Resources," in E. A. Engelbert and A. F. Scheuring, eds. *Water Scarcity: Impacts on Western Agriculture*, Berkeley, CA: University of CA Press, 1984, pp. 17-44.

Calthorpe, Peter and William Fulton, *The Regional City: Planning for the End of Sprawl*, Washington DC: Island Press, 2000.

Costanza, Robert, *et al.*, "The Value of the World's Ecosystem Services and Natural Capital," *Nature*, 387:253-260, May 15, 1997.

Cray, Dan, "Water War: A real estate developer's scheme to build a lake in a desert region seemed ludicrous. But maybe he's not all wet," *TIME*, July 30, 2001, "Bonus" section on Your Business, Y11.

Daily, Gretchen C., *Nature's Services: Societal Dependence on Natural Ecosystems*, Washington, DC: Island Press, 1997.

Dunn, Seth, *Hydrogen Futures: Toward a Sustainable Energy System*, Worldwatch paper 157, Washington DC: Worldwatch Institute, August 2001.

Eisenberg, Evan, *The Ecology of Eden*, New York: Alfred Knopf, 1998.

Elkington, John, *Cannibals With Forks: The Triple Bottom Line of 21st Century Business*, Gabriola Island, BC: New Society Publishers, 1998 (first published Oxford, 1997).

Fairley, Peter, "Fill 'er Up with Hydrogen," *Technology Today*, November-December 2000, pp. 54-62.

Gleick, P. H., *et al.*, *California Water 2020: A Sustainable Vision*, Oakland CA: Pacific Institute for Studies in Development, Environment, and Security, 1995.

Hawken, Paul, Amory Lovins, and L. Hunter Lovins, *Natural Capitalism: Creating the Next Industrial Revolution*, Boston: Little, Brown & Company, 1999.

Lavendel, Brian, "GreenHouse," *Audubon*, March-April 2001, pp. 75-78.

McDonough, William and M. Braungart, "The Next Industrial Revolution," *Atlantic Monthly*, 282 (4), October 1998.

Motavalli, Jim, "Zero Waste," *E: The Environmental Magazine*, March/April 2001, pp. 26-33.

Naar, Jon, "The Future Comes to Electrolux," *ONEARTH* (formerly *The Amicus Journal*) vol. 23 no. 3, fall 2001, pp. 34-37.

Rathje, W. and C. Murphy, *Rubbish! The Archeology of Garbage*, New York: HarperCollins, 1992.

Roston, Eric, "Warming Up To Green," *TIME* March 19, 2001, Business Section, B9.

Schumacher, E. F., *Small Is Beautiful: Economics As If People Mattered*, Introduction by Theodore Roszak, New York: Harper and Row, 1973.

Stahel, W. R. and G. Reday-Mulvey, *Jobs for Tomorrow: The Potential for Substituting Manpower for Energy*, New York: Vantage Press, 1981.

Weber, B., "At the Dump, Wish You Were Here," *New York Times*, March 27, 1996.

Womack, J. P. and D. T. Jones, "Beyond Toyota: How to root Out Waste and Pursue Perfection," *Harvard Business Review*, September-October 1996, pp. 140-158.

Womack, J. P. and Jones, D. T., *Lean Thinking: Banish Waste and Create Wealth in Your Corporation*, New York: Simon & Schuster, 1996.

World Bank: reports of 1995 *(Monitoring Environmental Progress: A Report on a Work in Progress)*, and 1997 *(Expanding the Measure of Wealth: Indicators of Environmentally Sustainable Development)* Environmentally Sustainable Development (Studies and Monographs) World Bank, Washington, DC.

Zeller, Tom, "Personally Empowered," *New York Times*, February 25, 2001, p. WK 16.

chapter three

Stewardship:
The Responsible Person

HOPE, DESPAIR, AND ACCEPTANCE

The previous chapter ended on a note of hope, of very justified hope. There are easier and better ways of doing what we are doing—driving to work, living in houses, taking out the trash. If we can simply put these easier, better, cheaper, more beautiful, and more sustainable practices into place, we will not have to worry about the future of the earth or the place of humans on the earth. With no blank checks written on the future, with only the technology presently in our possession, we can achieve sustainability at the highest standard of living, and teach the world to follow us. The major problems of our day will yield to elegant and easy solutions.

But there are catch phrases in all the solutions—maybe we should say, catch-22 phrases. Consider this:

> *If the rich countries replaced* part of their feedlot beef consumption with range beef and lamb, white meats, aquaculture, marine fish, or vegetable proteins, then Central and South America might feel less pressure to convert rainforest to pasture. Many developing countries could free up arable land. There could be less displacement of the rural poor onto marginal land, less soil erosion, and renewed emphasis on traditional food crops rather than on export cash crops.

This one action could save enough grain, *if properly distributed*, to feed the world's half billion hungry people.[1]

There is a terrible gap between the hypothetical and the probable. There are, for instance, many excellent reasons to cut back on our consumption of beef. But where the outcry should be, I hear ominous silence, broken only by the worldwide munching of McDonald's hamburgers, now the most popular food on earth. I can follow the causal chain that the authors have in mind, but when has any such action had any such effect? Did the radical decrease in cigarette smoking in the United States have any noticeable effect on tobacco fields? What was it? What makes anyone think that the benefits, if any, of this change, will be properly distributed?

> Such a replacement of annual grains with perennial cereals that do not require annual tilling and replanting could eliminate up to half the soil erosion in the United States, saving nearly $20 billion worth of U.S. soil and $9 billion worth of fuel for farm equipment every year. *If Jackson's ambitious research goal can be widely commercialized*, a bigger and more daunting step, then at least in the earth's great grasslands, farming may ultimately come to look as if nothing at all is happening.[2]

All that is required for the hypothesis to become reality is that people should learn what it is in their interest to learn, and then do, individually and collectively, what it is obviously in their interest, short term and long term, to do. Why does hollow laughter sound through the breaks after every paragraph?

Why do we not strive to change the world? Why do we not, usually, even write our Congressman about the rational changes that are needed to change the world? There is a paralysis that accompanies the transition from the present, which is tolerable if not good, and the future, which could be spectacular. (There is a paralysis because, if only we do nothing, we will be dead before all the horrible consequences of doing nothing appear on the earth.) The hypotheticals all say, if only we could all do *this*, where *this* is some simple thing, obviously reasonable, then a much better condition would result. But we don't do *this*, individually or collectively. We do not do it individually because we know that we will not do it collectively, and the better condition will not result unless we do it collectively. In some sense, we obey, very faithfully, some despairing empirical translation of Kant's normative Categorical Imperative: instead of, act only on that maxim that you can simultaneously will to become universal law, or "do only what you would want everyone to do," it becomes, act not on any maxim where the universal law is highly unlikely, or "do not do what you know everyone will not do (no matter how good it would be for everyone to do it)." There is no logic in this transition. Granted that, "If everyone did this, a better condition would result," from "But everyone won't do this," nothing follows. (That's called "denying the antecedent," and in logic, it gets you nowhere.)

But this logic has powerful empirical political precedent. In policy studies, we recognize two types of instability in collective arrangements that tax, or otherwise place a burden upon, the individual for the public good. In the first type of instability, the individual who defects from the arrangement gains an advantage vis-à-vis all the others, at any time that he defects; he enjoys all the benefits of the collective arrangement without having to bear the burden. There is therefore an incentive for every individual to cheat. In the second type of instability, the individual, or small group of individuals, who adhere to the arrangement, the others defecting, gain nothing; they suffer the burden of the arrangement but enjoy none of the benefits. There is therefore no incentive for any individual to assume the required burden in the absence of assurance that all the others will too. Any number of collective arrangements could be chosen to illustrate these instabilities. Taxation is the classic example; if I default on my taxes, I still enjoy police and fire protection and the use of the public schools, while I save my money. That is why we have tax collectors. If I pay my taxes, and my neighbors do not pay theirs, I lose my money but there will not be enough in the public till to pay for the benefits, so I gain nothing. That is why I am *glad* we have tax collectors. On the international scene, most treaties (for instance, disarmament treaties) exhibit both sorts of instability. On the environmental scene, almost all pollution abatement agreements do the same. Each company, or individual, must incur the cost of abatement in his own domain, but the public good of clean air or water will not be enjoyed unless everyone does the same. Unlike tax laws, pollution abatement laws are notoriously difficult to enforce. As far as the feedlot beef is concerned, I could become the most perfect vegetarian—my whole family could become the most perfect vegetarians—and we would not have the slightest effect on the pattern of meat consumption in America, let alone on the pasturelands in Ecuador and the rainforests in Brazil. Indeed, many have already done this, to no effect—at least, not of that type. We will return to this point.

So there is some reason behind my individual unwillingness to spend my very limited resources of time and energy on an enterprise that can yield no benefits unless everyone cooperates in it. For our purposes, in the attempt to work out a personal moral imperative that yields environmental sustainability, the task is now twofold. First, on the assumption that the normal presumption of the new literature of environmentally friendly capitalism is correct, that we are talking about benefits that will only be achieved if a solid majority *changes* in some significant way, we will explore, very briefly, the painful topic of negation: why that solid majority never changes in that way. Second, the conclusion of that discussion must be that any change for the better must work on individual terms as well as collective—the change must be good for the individual, for the individual's own advantage, in some way that does not depend on popular approval. In the end, there is no day but today, and no life but mine, that I can live. The argument to live the individual life of environmental sustainability, the life of simplicity in allegiance to the land, must not depend on general acceptance and the wonderful consequences foreseen in the last chapter. A concluding section will link this second exploration back with Chapter 1, and the search for a virtuous life in accordance with a personal moral imperative that includes responsibility for the land as part of itself.

THE FALLACY OF RATIONAL UTILITARIANISM

Jeremy Bentham (see Chapter 1) was logical, clear, and intuitively correct. We operate, except for rare bursts of altruism, in pursuit of pleasure and in avoidance of pain. We are capable (as adults) of foregoing immediate pleasure for the sake of obtaining more pleasure in the long run; we are capable (as a community) of selecting collective solutions that work out for the best interest of the majority, even if the temporary minority will have to suffer setbacks. Human behavior in the large scale and the long run is to be seen as the systematic pursuit of human interest.

Of course humans may be deceived as to their real interests (Bentham took aim at certain institutions, like the Church, that seemed to specialize in selling humans a false view of what is in their interest and what is not.) But as soon as people are freed, by the Enlightenment Spirit and science, from the superstitions of the past, they will be able to perceive their real interests, and the society as a whole will reinforce the individual inclination to do everything only to promote his own interest.

That is very logical. But that is not what he does. Let us join Fyodor Dostoevsky in his meditations from underground.

> Oh, tell me, who was it first announced, who was it first proclaimed, that man only does nasty things because he does not know his own interests; and that if he were enlightened, if his eyes were opened to his real normal interests, man would at once cease to do nasty things, would at once become good and noble because, being enlightened and understanding his real advantage, he would see his own advantage in the good and nothing else, and we all know that not one man can, consciously, act against his own interests, consequently, so to say, through necessity, he would begin doing good? Oh, the babe! Oh, the pure, innocent child! Why, in the first place, when in all these thousands of years has there been a time when man has acted only from his own interest? What is to be done with the millions of facts that bear witness that men, *consciously*, that is fully understanding their real interests, have left them in the background and have rushed headlong on another path, to meet peril and danger, compelled to this course by nobody and by nothing, . . and have obstinately, wilfully, struck out another difficult, absurd way, . . So, I suppose, this obstinacy and perversity were pleasanter to them than any advantage.[3]

Can we think of examples of this failure of rational self-interest that might be relevant to the discussion in Chapter 2? Can we ever. It is difficult to pick a starting point. Shall we start with the McDonald's hamburger, mentioned before? McDonald's is not unique; most "fast food" shares the high-calorie, high-fat, high-cholesterol characteristics that make obesity the most significant cause of mortality and morbidity on the American scene. The fascination with that hamburger rapidly destroys the remaining rainforests of the world; it homogenizes all local tastes into an internationally accepted amalgam, destroying local culture along the way; and it is terribly expensive, in price per pound of nourishment and in trash disposal requirements. It is not an economical choice for anyone. And it will kill us; it contributes to our death from heart disease, stroke (and the other physical consequences of hypertension), type II diabetes, and probably cancer. We sing the praises of individualistic selfishness, and the freedom to live our lives as we want to live them, but we do not live as if our lives, even our physical lives, mattered to us.

And if our eating habits betray a puzzling inattention to rational interests, what can we say about our advertising, possibly the best barometer of popular culture? Recall, for instance, the admirable experiment in car sharing reported in Chapter 2. The reasoning is impeccable. Why do we want a car? To get us from here to there, maybe in style, maybe with the living room furniture in the rear somehow, maybe with six children on the way to the soccer game. Why *own* all those cars, or settle for just one that can do only one of those things? Join a car sharing group and have access to many different kinds of vehicles, at a much lower price. How sensible! Now consider the currently running television advertisement for a popular midsize car. To the tune of "Raindrops Keep Falling On My Head," a very undistinguished man (pudgy, balding) stands in his driveway in the pouring rain with a beatific smile on his face, admiring his new shiny car. It is not the car's services he values. It is that car in his driveway. The examples of such portrayals could be multiplied, including owners who sleep in the garage so they can reach out and touch their cars in the middle of the night, owners who drive slowly through their neighborhoods while neighbors faint from envy, owners who pretend not to know the car is theirs so they can enjoy being reminded—and more of the same. Half the automobile advertisements you can think of describe not the services of the car or (especially) SUV, but, as it were, its *disservices*: how it makes you feel proud; how it towers over the other cars on the block, intimidating their owners;[4] how it makes you feel like you're ramming through the bushes, wrecking the groundcover, destroying mountains; how it, in short, encourages all the anti-social, proud, sinful, and perverse motivations you can access. (My favorite advertisement, set in a men's locker room, shows the assault to his manhood felt by a man when he is identified as owning a minivan, when everyone else owns an SUV.)

It is tempting to stay with the cars, for they, or rather their images, adhere so closely to the consumer's image of himself, and because they dominate America's image of itself. But there are so many more examples of why the rational, easy course is not for us. We claim to appreciate the good and the durable, yet our shoe repairmen are going out of business. The inexpensive shoes, and mostly sneakers, that we buy, are all manmade materials and cannot be repaired. (In other contexts we would be tempted to add, that they are all made abroad, and usually by the labor of women and children making at most $1 per day.) When they wear through, which they quickly do, there is nothing to do but throw them in the landfill. An art, the shoemaker's and shoe repairer's art, is dying, and there is nothing we can do to keep it in existence, except to buy the kinds of shoes, well made of good materials, that endure and can be repaired, and as already described there is no point in doing it unless everybody does.

Another example is the mall. "Shopping" used to be an instrumental term: There is something we need, so we shop around (go from shop to shop in the market) to get the best type at the lowest cost. "Going shopping" recreationally was one of the weirder perquisites of the carriage trade. But now the mall is the center of life for many of us, and "shopping" is a central activity. It is part of the Mall ethic that shoes no longer can be repaired. No product must be sold, according to what we may call the Retail Imperative, that cannot be thrown out soon, so that others may be bought. The experience of "going shopping," of going to the mall, of feasting eyes and imagination on display after display of new, untouched things, of picking out, of holding the new thing, clutching it, thinking of enjoying it, thinking of showing it off, proud and happy to own it—this is the experience that we seek.

Grasping the new thing produces a kind of "high," or rush, exhilaration, some culminating experience for the American of the mall culture, and anticipation of that high is almost better than the climax itself. It is certainly not the "service" of the thing that we seek. As a matter of fact, when the showing-off period is over and it begins to render whatever service it was supposed to have been bought for, we immediately discover its deficiencies, since it was hardly designed for good service. Fortunately, it will not last long, and as soon as it stops working, or frays, or tears away from its sole, we will have a reason to go back to the mall and begin the whole pleasurable experience all over again. There will be no regret; it didn't cost very much.

The familiar situation, as described, is simply perverse. Consider its harm. Nonrenewable resources have been extracted from the earth to provide the basis for its materials (probably some sort of petroleum–based materials). In the makeshift factory in which the object was assembled, the surrounding earth and water were recruited and then fouled as part of the manufacture. Given its price, we cannot assume any scrupulous environmental controls on the throughput and waste disposal of the manufacturing process. (In this context, we will ignore the exploitation and poverty of the workers who assembled it.) Fossil fuel was further expended in transporting to our shores the containers in which it was packed, then by the trucks that brought it to the mall. The mall itself is one huge exercise in lighting, heating, and air-conditioning spaces, with no motivation (and given its scale, probably no possibility) for environmentally sound design. Everything about the product—its design, manufacture, and display for sale—inclines it to be purchased shortly after its arrival in the store, used briefly, and discarded to make room for others, a huge societal throughput engineered to expend resources and fill landfills as rapidly as possible. This product—shoe, radio, toy, whatever—is a direct assault on the natural capital of the earth. As such, it involves the cooperative purchaser in that assault, and makes him a collaborator in the crime. To the extent that the purchaser is minimally aware of the environmental consequences of the material culture in which he participates, he is guilty of formal cooperation in a matter that is clearly wrong.

Worse yet, he initiates his children into this material maze, ensuring that they will acquire all the wrong habits of mind where material goods are concerned. This initiation is only with great difficulty reconciled with our stated desires for our children—that they be intellectually curious, physically fit, and morally strong—and our certain knowledge, dating back to Aristotle, that early exposures make all the difference in moral development. Can it be right to allow them to be part of this consumer madness?

Yet the consumer never stipulated for evil. We cannot credit him with originality in engaging in wrongful behavior. He is simply caught up in the world that matter has made, as part of a materialist culture. The shortcomings of this culture have been pointed out with such eloquence and vigor, in so many excellent best-selling works, from the mid-1950s to this day, that it would be unrealistic to assume that he never even heard of the possibility of living differently (and folly to use these pages to compete.)[5] *Natural Capitalism* is only one of the more recent of these, unique for its optimism and the practicality of its positive prescriptions. Can there be any explanation of why, in this most self-interested of civilizations, simple self-interest does not seem to have any commanding sway in the conduct of our collective life?

One explanation of the curious national schizophrenia—living the material life while praising the works that condemn it—is by way of analogy. Those who study infants tell us that the moments in which an infant learns—learns everything from which breast is its mother's to which foot is its own—are the rare "quiet-alert" moments, when the infant is neither so hungry or sore that it must scream until its needs are met, nor so sleepy that it cannot focus. Fortunately for the human race, the infant can use these "quiet-alert" moments to learn everything it needs to know to be an infant. We adults, too, have such moments, when we can reflect at leisure, with full attention, on what the rational course of our lives must include. Well–fed and well–rested, exposed to such rational arguments as *Natural Capitalism* and similar literature musters, we may confidently orient ourselves to a much more reasonable life—the future of the natural world seems to require it and it is, in any case, in accord with our best interests. The intentions are good. But let the moment pass, and the whole weight of the material culture again descends upon us. Truth is, it is impossible to maintain a life solely on the strength of its rationality. It is futile to maintain a life in a way that *would* have marvelous effects on the whole destiny of the earth and the human race, if only everyone would live that way, which they won't. It is terribly difficult to maintain a life even if the only goal is individual advantage as appreciated by others—good health and good looks in the long run, for instance—if to live that way flies in the face of every tendency of the civilization around us. (Consider the success rate of regimes of diet and exercise.) The path of least resistance will always be toward the life portrayed in the most popular advertisements.

In the midst of a material culture, the only way to develop a stance against it is to adopt a moral imperative that centers on our own lives alone, but that also responds to that culture. This stance must be so compellingly powerful that it can stand as a viable alternative to the culturally accepted choices for an individual life. To that enterprise we now turn.

SIMPLICITY

"I went to the woods," Henry David Thoreau said, "because I wanted to live deliberately." What would it be to live deliberately? In Thoreau's meaning, we find the stipulation in Chapter 1, that the good life, when we find it, will be a life lived on a principle of reason, a rational life. In his choice of the means for achieving that end, we find the essential role of the natural environment, the wilderness, in discovering that life. Thoreau does not say at that point (but does elsewhere) that getting away from the neighbors, and from all other instrumentalities of the dominant trend of the society, may be essential for living the deliberate life, at least for discovering it at its outset. We are social animals, after all. If the neighbors help us live a rational life, it will be that much easier to live. If the neighbors cannot comprehend such a life, which is more likely, they will make it that much more difficult. If the neighbors are compounded by the television, the mall, and the Web, it may be very difficult to achieve that distance from them that would provide a truly independent perspective and the "quiet-alert" moments to appreciate it. Hence the need to get away from it all, to be alone.

Let us start with the conceptual challenge. We need to describe a life that works to counter individual wastefulness in a culture both individualistic and wasteful. Given the criteria laid down in Chapter 1—especially that we must live a life centering on virtue, and characterized by deliberation and choice—and the possibilities outlined in Chapter 2, can we now describe a good individual life, one lived in allegiance with the land? We can, and its name is simplicity. This virtue brings together the tangled threads of our demands upon the intellectual tradition.

The purpose of this chapter is to discover the virtue that can form the central content of a personal worldview for any person interested in living a good life, regardless of whether the world is interested in going along with it. Simplicity is its name, and it has meant many things, but always *in opposition to* some condition understood to be prevalent in our civilizations, a condition identified as multiplicity, and apparently perfectly incorporated in the Mall.

"Simplicity" in its abundant literature seems to be woven of several distinguishable strands (although no actual account separates them). They generally reinforce each other, like any good braid; yet in practice, they represent different emphases and agendas. **Spiritual simplicity** offers the resolution of the tensions within the human soul into an ordered unity experienced as personal serenity; **cultural simplicity**, the rejection of the individualist competition and distraction of modern life in favor of simple community; **political simplicity**, the rejection of corporate exploitation of the poor in the form of economic imperialism and war in favor of a life close to the land and dedicated to world justice; **economic simplicity**, the rejection of fast-track jobs and high-profile consumption in favor of a slower pace of life, lower income and lower spending, more time for family and neighborhood; and finally **environmental simplicity**, the rejection of the high-consumption high-waste lifestyles of the developed world, in favor of a life that will leave as light as possible a footprint on the earth. For clarity's sake, we now give a brief account of each.

Spiritual Simplicity

Spiritual simplicity has a long and honorable history, beginning in Plato and perfected in the Church. According to Raoul Plus, a Jesuit Scholar writing in the 1950s (before any hint of politics entered the discussion), the ideal of simplicity begins with the simplicity of God, and is defined negatively as the absence of duality, complexity, or contradiction. As St. Vincent de Paul put it, God is "a sole being, one and uncompounded. We must strive to become in virtue what God is in nature."[6] "God alone: nothing in the eternal simplicity of God is changed."[7] Humans introduced division into the world, with their sin, and caused the conflict that we experience as our senses (and bodily desires) in revolt against the spirit. Now we must put down that revolt in order to be one person again.[8] Christians take as their example Jesus, who chose a simple lifestyle, content with absolute poverty, just to make his message clear to people who are likely to get confused. He was never distracted by anything created. "Beatitude is promised to those who love nothing save God, desire only God, judge events only in relation to God—the triumph of that fundamental simplicity."[9]

Plus insists that the simplicity sought by the Christian is the simplicity of small children, who in all things are absolutely honest, and act without reflection or pretense. We may set aside the monk's ignorance of the child's mind; the point is clear. The person who has achieved simplicity proceeds right on without turning left or right or spending time in introspection. "He who is simple forgets about himself, and without having to make an effort at self-forgetfulness."[10] Simplicity is therefore very different from the virtue of humility, which is cautious, always watching her step, and self-evaluating all the time. Simplicity is straightforward, fixed on the object of action. It avoids both attention to reputation, which examines every action for its praiseworthiness, and excess humility, which examines every action for blameworthiness. The point is to accept praise and blame with equanimity, and get on with what you're doing.

The simplicity developed with God in prayer, which comes down to the single acceptance of God's love, is expressed also in relation to our neighbor, as absolute honesty, the lack of hypocrisy or pretense, and again, an absence of self-consciousness (which immediately entails duality). Now that the neighbor and the community are brought into the equation, it is important to think of the support we give that neighbor in his own efforts at simplicity, and therefore of how the externals of dress, dwelling, and habits of consumption may express the simple life. The person who practices simplicity, Plus thinks, will develop a good, because simple, spiritual life, in the simple relation of son to father. He will also be best adapted to deal with unexpected situations that come up, since he has more flexibility and freedom than most, for he has few material possessions to distract him and demand care.

For Plus, spiritual simplicity is a joyful state, fresh, spontaneous, untroubled. He admits that it is a very small part of religious training now, and hardly present in the Church. Instead, the present (Baltimore Catechism) constant attention to rules and sin make people "scrupulous," so preoccupied with their own failings that they cannot relate to themselves, others, or God, without dividing themselves into actor and censor, perpetually chewing themselves up. He concludes that we should yet strive for simplicity, understood as a completely undivided soul.

Yet there is a point that Plus misses. How do we create ourselves as the people we want to be? Plus to the contrary, there is one form of psychological dualism necessary in any account of the virtues, including this one. Recall Chapter 1, and Aristotle's explanation on how we become virtuous. First we practice, according to rule, the acts (behavior) appropriate to the virtue we are to acquire—we volunteer to bring things to people who need them according to the rule of "compassion," we stand up against the bully according to the rule of "courage," and so forth. We cannot become a compassionate or courageous person without such practice, and to guide the practice, Aristotle has no better advice than "to perform the [just] action as a just man would perform it." So while our days of virtue are still far off, we *act as if* we were a person with the requisite virtue, and it is by acting that way that we acquire the virtue. Is this hypocrisy? No; it is self-directed growth. Like the chambered nautilus of poetic fame, we create the shell of the person we want to be, then grow into the shell by adopting the role of that person. The trouble is, as Plus points out, that hypocrisy (like self-examination) of the harmless sort, carried on for a particular limited purpose, becomes habit-forming, and generalizes to a dualistic life, where I am always at once myself and the person I am pretending to be. So we must be on the watch for the dissembling life to grow out of the adolescent trying of roles. Adolescence is good, but only if it ends in adulthood.

This process of growing into a definition also highlights another temptation to which Plus addresses himself, the temptation to acquire a set of material goods to fit each of many definitions. One reason the material exterior of the self—the clothing, jewelry, hair, general manner—is important is that we use it to define the self. If I am a certain sort of person, I will choose a certain style in all I have, wear, and possess—household furnishings, personal transportation, clothes, leisure activities, and the like. These externals are the *equipment* that I need to be that person, as one needs certain equipment to climb a mountain. My equipment signals to others, and reminds me of, the kind of person I am. Now if, in response to a multiplicity of incompatible demands, I choose to be several people at once, I will have to purchase the equipment for each of those people—the hard–working professional, the dedicated gardener, the competent handyman, the rugged mountain explorer, the fashionable nightclubber—and that can lead to a good many purchases of equipment, most of which will be used seldom, since it belongs to a person I cannot often be. Indeed, if there is a person I want to be, but cannot be at present for lack of time or training, I may take on the image of that person simply by purchasing the equipment. If I own this equipment, the mind reasons to itself, I must be the person that needs it, which is the person I (sometimes) want to be. For this reason professional women collect cookbooks they never open, and garden tools they never wield; professional men buy expensive sneakers, extra-light outdoor parkas and shorts, and other equipment for climbing roadless mountains, which they do not do (consider the SUV, again). Step one toward simplicity of material existence, clearly, is the choice of which of the many fantasies of ourselves we really intend to live, and the firm abandonment of the others.

There is another stage, or type, of dualism built into the choice of the simple life—in that, very simply, I am *choosing* that life. Thoreau went to the woods, recall, because he wanted to live *deliberately*, a life he had chosen upon deliberation. In other literature we are called upon to live *consciously, intentionally,* or *voluntarily*; these are all the same. That means, in logic, there must be a chooser and a chosen for, and while they may extensionally be the same, they differ in meaning—at least at the moment of choice, I am subject and object both. That's not very simple, and it seems to contradict Plus' notion of the ideal artless simplicity of the child. In terms of psychological simplicity, the entire process of reflection upon one's own life and choice to change it is a choice *away from* the non-reflective simplicity of the truly thoughtless. For that reason alone, we will have to reject the notion of "primitive, childlike" simplicity as model. Intentional living, whatever else it may turn out to mean, surely means a life lived as maturely chosen by the one who lives it.

That choice is the focus of the first part of Duane Elgin's *Voluntary Simplicity*, a transition work from the spiritual to the other forms of simplicity. As Elgin points out, the "choices" that we make as consumers up to our ears in a consumer society often cannot be called real "choices" at all, springing as they do from the latest advertising hype laid upon lifetime layers of unconscious conditioning to the material society. Most of the time, we run on automatic. Most of the time, our minds are filled with the roar and shouts of half-conscious fantasies. This is the "stream of consciousness" behind which we must find our own selves, hidden and quiet. Every major religious tradition (Christianity included, Elgin to the contrary notwithstanding) has insisted upon this effort to discover the core of the self, in order that the choice of a life to be lived may be genuine.[11]

The process of discovery, or discernment, of that core, the life we are best suited to live, is the search for **vocation**. Our vocation, literally, what we are *called* to do, is the life for which we are best fitted by nature, and which will call forth our best and highest abilities. (This account follows Parker Palmer, in his 2000 *Let Your Life Speak*.) It is not necessarily the life we have adopted, even according to our highest and best values, as instructed by others. We cannot will ourselves into a vocation. It waits for us, and we learn about it not by doing but by listening.

> [Our lives] speak through our actions and reactions, our intuitions and instincts, our feelings and bodily states of being, perhaps more profoundly than through our words. We are like plants, full of tropisms that draw us toward certain experiences and repel us from others. If we can learn to read our own responses to our own experience—a text we are writing unconsciously every day we spend on earth—we will receive the guidance we need to live more authentic lives.[12]

The vocation is the ultimate simplifier for life, because it identifies the one thing that we should be doing and being. Once we know that, we don't need to waste time dividing our energies among the many activities a complex civilization demands of all the people we are fantasizing and trying to be, let alone accumulating the equipment for lives we no longer need to pretend to live. This notion of vocation is different from some in the tradition, for the voice that calls is not external—God in some heaven—but within, from the nature with which, whatever our ideas of creation, we arrived on this earth. It takes a certain amount of faith to believe that within ourselves, without our creating it, there is a spark of the Divine waiting to be discerned and lived out, regardless of the strongest desires of the people we follow and admire, regardless, really, of our own desires. Yet it has a traditional heritage. There is a Hasidic tale, that "Rabbi Zusya, when he was an old man, said, 'In the coming world, they will not ask me: "Why were you not Moses?" They will ask me: "Why were you not Zusya?[13]" ' " The point is not to be the ultimate hero, but to be ourselves. We will know when we get there because, very simply, we will be happy.

> Our deepest calling is to grow into our own authentic selfhood, whether or not it conforms to some image of who we *ought* to be. As we do so, we will not only find the joy that every human being seeks—we will also find our path of authentic service in the world. True vocation joins self and service, as Frederick Buechner asserts when he defines vocation as "the place where your deep gladness meets the world's deep need."[14]

Finding our vocation, and choosing to follow it, revolves specifically on our cultivation of a natural aspect of dualism: the fact that we are not only actors, we are witnesses to (and commentators upon!) our actions. That witness capability, what Plus refers to as "self-examination" (that must be restrained from spilling over into scrupulosity), what Palmer calls "discernment," must be encouraged and refined. To know our habitual and automatic patterns of thought and reaction is to be free of them—free to follow them wholeheartedly and intentionally, if they are good, and free to set them aside if they are hindering more than helping. Ultimately, this capacity for reflection must be developed into a finely tuned instrument of discernment, so that we may tell the true choices from the false ones.

By one strand of the tradition, as Duane Elgin points out, the discovery of the true self is accompanied by the simultaneous discovery that there is no real boundary between self and world, and that consciousness contains the universe.[15] Elgin also picks up a theme that we brought out in the first chapter: the decision to make our life intentional, to make it our own, is obligatory. We are conscious responsible beings, capable of choosing our lives and the principles by which we will live them, and for that reason alone we ought to do that; there is an imperative to adopt a personal moral worldview.[16]

Cultural Simplicity

The Christian commitment to spiritual simplicity, described by Plus, took an early turn to the community. Benedict of Nursia, founder of one of the first, and certainly the most influential, permanent Christian monasteries at Monte Cassino, began his religious life as a hermit, seeking God in solitude. But he became convinced, especially as followers insisted on seeking him out in his cave, that only in community, in the practice of brotherly love and Christian charity, could the ideal of spiritual perfection be realized.[17] The doctrine of the Trinity portrays God as social by nature; Christ stressed that service to others was service to him—we are clearly meant to live in community, which must be a school for the spiritual life. Benedict's famous Rule, a model of commonsensical guidance for people trying to live together, created an environment where monks could practice charity and yet spend enough time in solitary prayer to achieve spiritual fulfillment.

Palmer puts this necessary move in contemporary terms:

> The Quaker teacher Douglas Steere was fond of saying that the ancient human question "Who am I?" leads inevitably to the equally important question "Whose am I?"—for there is no selfhood outside relationship. . . . As I learn more about the seed of true self that was planted when I was born, I also learn more about the ecosystem in which I was planted—the network of communal relations in which I am called to live responsively, accountably, and joyfully with beings of every sort. Only when I know both seed and system, self and community, can I embody the great commandment to love both my neighbor and myself.[18]

The turn to community within the Christian religious tradition not only allowed a more adequate notion of what a monk must do to be saved, it created a powerful institution. The monastic movement dominated Christianity through the centuries that followed Monte Cassino. The monasteries, through the Dark Ages of Europe, were the only repository of learning, keepers of the books and founders of schools; they were also, for better and for worse, exemplars of the virtues and problems of community. Following the traditional single-sex vowed communities, a series of lay religious communities, starting with the Anabaptists, modeled themselves on the early Christian Church (described in the Acts of the Apostles), where the Brethren lived together, dedicated all their property to the community, and shared all their lives in common.

America has long been the home of Communitarian movements that took collective simplicity as their central social value. At least in their own understandings, the founders of our original settlements—the Separatists of 1620, the Puritans of Massachusetts Bay in 1628—came to these shores to found intentional communities, to live according to religious values radically different from those of the societies they had left behind, and in so doing to show the world that it was, indeed, possible to live this way. Commercial motives, while present from the start, were to take a distinct second place to the life of worship and simplicity. They strongly believed that God wanted them to live that way. In that line may be found the radical Protestant communities (Amish, Mennonite), direct descendants of the

Anabaptists, that persist to this day in the "plain" life that they believe is commanded by Scripture and by their tradition. "Intentional" communities, part of a vigorous and deliberate anarchist move to create a culture apart from the materialism and vulgarity of industrial society, sprang up in the rural areas of the United States in the 19th century; Brook Farm, where Nathaniel Hawthorne lived for awhile, and the Oneida Community of upstate New York state, were among the better known.

The movement revived in the 1960s and 1970s, in response to the increasingly chaotic and threatening militarism of Cold War America. The most stable and successful of these '60s communities was (usefully for our purposes) based not on religious principles but on the tenets of B. F. Skinner's behavioral psychology as laid down in his account of the fictional community *Walden II*, and was established specifically to create a more rational and human-friendly community. Twin Oaks, in Louisa, Virginia, was founded in 1967 to provide a setting where people could live and raise their families according to the values of cooperation, sharing, nonviolence, equality, and ecology; they are going strong to this day, and their webpage will tell you how to get their newsletters and arrange for a tour of the community.[19] What is extraordinary about the Twin Oaks community is its very survival through (by now) three generations; the secular Intentional Community movement, however powerfully its proponents were originally attracted to it, rarely established lasting settlements. The life was hard, friends and family did not understand, and it is very difficult to keep any group of people working together, without flying apart at the seams, absent some very strong material motivation (like the need to make a living) or, as in a traditional monastery, a strong religious faith.

Political Simplicity

During the same decades of the 20th century, the pursuit of simplicity took a political form in response to global injustice and the Cold War. The Christian Simple Living movement, as it was called, extended through the 1970s, dedicated not only to seeking the Christian simple life, but also to the pursuit of global economic justice, the defense of pacifism, and an ethic of cooperation, and, for the first time, the preservation of the threatened earth. It joined, in effect, a global political agenda to the cultural defense of the simple life against the selfish materialism, militarism, and wastefulness of the society of the time.[20] The signers of the Shakertown Pledge, formulated and adopted by a group of pastors and retreat directors in the spring of 1973, fully intended to change the world, not only themselves. The provisions of the pledge (opposite page), such as requiring its signers to share their wealth with the poor, are not intended to help them achieve spiritual purity through some "holy poverty" ("a St. Francis trip," as one of them put it), but to help feed the poor, who need the food. As Adam Finnerty, one of the signers, explained,

The Shakertown Pledge

Recognizing that the earth and the fulness thereof is a gift from our gracious God, and that we are called to cherish, nurture, and provide loving stewardship for the earth's resources,

and recognizing that life itself is a gift, and a call to responsibility, joy, and celebration,

I make the following declarations:

1. I declare myself to be a world citizen.

2. I commit myself to lead an ecologically sound life.

3. I commit myself to lead a life of creative simplicity and to share my personal wealth with the world's poor.

4. I commit myself to join with others in the reshaping of institutions in order to bring about a more just global society in which all people have full access to the needed resources for their physical, emotional, intellectual, and spiritual growth.

5. I commit myself to occupational accountability, and so doing I will seek to avoid the creation of products which cause harm to others.

6. I affirm the gift of my body and commit myself to its proper nourishment and physical well-being.

7. I commit myself to examine continually my relations with others, and to attempt to relate honestly, morally, and lovingly to those around me.

8. I commit myself to personal renewal through prayer, meditation, and study.

9. I commit myself to responsible participation in a community of faith.

We believe that an ecologically sound, creatively simple lifestyle is important for three reasons: first, so that our own lives can be more simple and gracious, freed from excessive attachment to material goods; second, so that we are able to release more of our wealth to share with those who need the basic necessities of life; third, so that we can begin to move toward a Just World Standard of Living, in which we are not consuming more of the earth's resources than is our due.[21]

The first reason is essentially the pursuit of spiritual simplicity; the second reason changes the end of that pursuit without changing the means (I desire and consume less, not to change myself but to give my neighbor more); and the third is frankly political, to use that simplicity as a manifesto and a means to changing the political structure of the western world.

We note that these "types" of simplicity are not only not mutually exclusive, but are in fact mutually supportive. The disciplined monk or saint has already renounced, and through a more difficult path, the individual materialistic strivings that separate people from community; the person who has lived for some formative time in a disciplined community is much readier to adopt the spiritual disciplines. Indeed, that is why monks went into community instead of remaining hermits on the model of the Desert Fathers. The political influence that the monks wielded through much of medieval Europe arose partly from the model of holiness that they embodied (and the religious services they provided) to the surrounding towns, but also partly from the wealth they commanded, amassed by the disciplined and skilled labors of workers who consumed very little of what they produced.

It is not unusual for the pursuit of personal integrity to issue in political action. Parker Palmer claims that the entire civil rights movement in the United States can be explained as the faithful living out of personal vocation. The movement was, he argues, created by different sorts of people, but they were alike in that they decided at one point to live faithfully. In their cases, the system threatened punishment if they did not agree to wear a mask, a mask of acceptance of the system.

> But in spite of that threat, or because of it, the people who plant the seeds of movements make a critical decision: they decide to live "divided no more." *They decide no longer to act on the outside in a way that contradicts some truth about themselves that they hold deeply on the inside.* They decide to claim authentic selfhood and act it out—and their decisions ripple out to transform the society in which they live, serving the selfhood of millions of others.[22]

That decision, the decision to stand where you really are instead of where someone else thinks you should be, he calls the "Rosa Parks decision," after the African-American bus passenger who refused to move to the back of the bus, and in refusing, launched the Montgomery Bus Boycott and the civil rights movement.

Economic Simplicity

Common sense suggests that consuming less has some advantages that have nothing to do with the monastic life; if you buy less, you need less money. Conversely, if you buy a great deal, or live very expensively in any way at all, you will have to have a great deal of money to support it. In this century, when few of us have inherited millions to support us without any effort on our part, obtaining a great deal of money usually requires working very long hours at an economically valuable high-technology and high-stress job, on top of an education lasting years into adulthood. The education focused so much on the future that it allowed little time to live in the present, and the job leaves little time for other things you might want to do with your life. The logic of economic simplicity is compelling: Limit your desires for material things, thereby reducing the need for all the money to buy them, and you will find that you do not have to work such long hours under such high stress. You will have more time for family, inexpensive recreation, neighbors, flowers, music, and all the other valuable things in life.

A move to embrace economic simplicity arose in the United States shortly after the stock market crash of 1987. That incident did very little permanent damage, but it sobered a generation accustomed to unbroken prosperity. As with most soberings, it surely appeared permanent at the time. As documented by Janice Castro in *TIME* magazine in 1991,

> After a 10-year bender of gaudy dreams and godless consumerism, Americans are starting to trade down. They want to reduce their attachments to status symbols, fast-track careers and great expectations of Having It All. Upscale is out; downscale is in. Yuppies are an ancient civilization.[23]

Not all Americans, of course, and the "trading down" often turned out to be more complicated than anyone had expected; see *TIME's* follow-up a decade later.[24] But the value themes that emerged in that self-conscious and very partial simplification reverberate through all the literatures on the topic.

> In place of materialism, many Americans are embracing simpler pleasures and homier values. They've been thinking hard about what really matters in their lives, and they've decided to make some changes. What matters is having time for family and friends, rest and recreation, good deeds and spirituality.[25]

The move seemed to stem in part from a strong feeling that life was going "too fast," that there was "too much" going on, a normal reaction against the objective changes brought about in American life by the enormous increase in the amount of information needed to conduct business in the globalizing economy and the instant access to that information through e-mail, fax, beeper, and cell-phone. It was easy to feel overwhelmed. It still is. We did not evolve in any such flood of information or such demand for instant processing of information, and part of us still longs for the village bard who could memorize, and repeat, all the information anyone in the village would ever need. More to the economic point, there was a strong feeling that life was filled up with too many "things," consumables, that living was being overwhelmed by "stuff" and all its demands. As a Hewlett-Packard manager put it, "I'm really sated with gadgets, things, adornments and all that stuff." More to the spiritual point, note that the new simplicity was the result of "thinking hard about what really matters"—as with all forms of the simple life, economic simplicity is conscious, deliberate, and intentional.

The rebellion against speed, stress, complexity, and stuff was reinforced by the early 1990s recession, which made a necessity of what the simplifiers had seen as virtue. Most Americans had not done well during the Reagan years; only the wealthiest 20 percent had actually gotten richer, and of the rest, the poorest had fallen farthest. "After adjustment for inflation," Castro wrote in 1991, "the national standard of living has actually fallen since 1973; the real average hourly pay for U.S. workers has gone from $8.55 then to $7.54 today."[26] It was also the era when the "yuppies" became the "sandwich generation," required to care for their aging parents while arranging for the education of their late-born children. Even consumer debt seemed to be easing; the plastic was relegated to a less-accessible place in the home. One result of the not-entirely-voluntary downsizing: The grand old full-service department stores, chain and local, quietly closed their doors as the new "big-box" discounters took over the clothing market.

But the central insight of this "movement," if such it was, was that the new careers were taking up far too much time and energy. Their parents' generation had worked a predictable eight hours a day at predictable jobs, traveled, except for the young sales force, rather little, and had time and energy in the evenings for family, choral groups, community service, and bowling leagues. Moreover, Mother usually stayed home, at least for the most part, and had time to go to school for plays, conferences, and volunteering at after-school activities. Those times seemed to be gone, and were missed.

Economic simplicity, as documented in this newsmagazine essay, has parallel strands in the other varieties. "Cocooning," as the stay-at-home trend was called, does not entail separation from the community, for instance. A part, if only a small part, of the move to the simpler economic life parallels cultural simplicity in its renunciation of the rat race for the sake of greater neighborliness. A part, if only an even smaller part, has to do with saving the environment. It also includes a desire for a heightened spiritual life. "Spirituality is in," theologian Martin Marty is quoted as saying; "so much so that I get embarrassed by it."[27]

Was it real? An interesting commentary on the move to economic simplicity came from Mark Burch a decade later, in his *Stepping Lightly*, an essay on the link between the simple life and sustainability (more on that in the next section). He points out that the major thrust of the 1990s simplifying had to do with, in effect, becoming independently wealthy: adjusting your financial picture and consumption habits together to ensure enough money to live the way you want to live without having to keep the high-stress job you dislike. For much of the movement, the "freedom" gained in simplicity was the "freedom" of money; "security" came from knowing that resources were sufficient for the pared-down lifestyle. Citing the popular "bible" of the economic simplicity movement, *Your Money or Your Life*, he points out that whether or not its authors intended, they "contribute to the idea that voluntary simplicity is mainly for those affluent enough to need financial planning assistance and fortunate enough to contemplate a day when they might receive an income without working for it."[28] Simplicity does bring freedom and security, he argues, but in an entirely different way. It is not just a clever way to make your money go further and satisfy all your desires for less; it is a redirection of desires, to minimize material wants altogether, so that contentment can be found without any special financial arrangements. In what amounts to a restatement of the conclusion of Book IX of Plato's *Republic*, Burch argues that the three major wants of human life—sufficiency, freedom, and security from fear—can be found in the simple life, far more than in the life of wealth and power.

Even at the time, the "simplification" move was dismissed as a fad by knowledgeable observers, a shallow flashback to the 1960s. That dismissal is validated by the disappearance of the move to economic simplicity in the revived Clinton economy that began in the next year. But the fact that it showed up at all, in proportions large enough for national recognition, is a reminder that it is a perpetual possibility, a rich stream still flowing, just beneath the surface of the hard-driving, hard-consuming, American way of life.

Environmental Simplicity

Environmental simplicity became an explicit possibility only in the last quarter of the 20th century, as we came to know the global threat to the environment posed by human activity. This phase of the move to simplicity is documented by Mark Burch in *Stepping Lightly: Simplicity for People and the Planet.* On the way to environmental simplicity, Burch reviews the stages of the simple life much as we have here. We begin with integrity, becoming one person:

> Simpler living begins when people become conscious of their values and live congruently with them, *whatever they may be* . . .Practitioners of voluntary simplicity begin from *questions* such as these: What do I value in life? How can I align my practice of daily living so that it brings me more into the presence of my values or expresses them more clearly? What in my life distracts me from this task or clutters my expression of these values, and how can I rid myself of it?[29]

Like Elgin, and Finnerty to a lesser extent, Burch never loses track of the fact that simplicity is a means only, but a means to several ends. New in Burch is the focus on the protection of the environment as a central end. He prefaces his discussion of the relationship between the life of simplicity and care for the natural environment with the familiar litany of environmental abuses that typified the last years of the 20th century, and show no signs of abating now—the ominous change in our climate, the loss of our forests, the devastation of our fisheries, and the appalling waste of fossil fuel and other resources, among other alarming signs of deterioration. His calculations, based on Wackernagel and Rees's concept of the "ecological footprint,"[30] are easy to remember. The authors set out to measure

> how much productive land and ocean is required to support one person at the typical North American standard of living. . . .[they] estimated that about 17.75 acres of land and productive ocean are required to support each North American, land that is either allocated to these uses on the North American continent or "appropriated" from other continents through the importation of resources or the "export" of wastes. [To] support *everyone* in the world at the North American standard . . . would require about 106.5 billion acres of land (6 billion people times 17.75 acres per person). The problem is, there are only 22.5 billion acres of productive land and ocean surface on the planet. Hence to realize the goal of a typical North American consumer lifestyle for everyone on Earth would require four extra planets *at the present time*.[31]

That's right now, of course. If we continue our present economic growth, at about 2.5 percent annually, our demand will double in about 28 years. There's eight planets we'll need. But we also expect the population of the world to continue to increase at about that rate, also doubling in 28 years. There's 16 planets we'll need.[32]

Calculated otherwise, the numbers are no more heartening. In 1986, it was estimated that humans had appropriated to their use some 40 percent of the Net Primary Production of the earth (the total product of photosynthesis). That percentage is increasing, leaving less and less for all the other species that depend on the same meat, fish, fiber, fruits, and leaves that we like. And as we churn out the pollution, we harm the very regenerative power of the earth, so even that level of Net Primary Production cannot be sustained.[33]

But the point is not the litany of despair, which can lead only to resignation (we can start singing the death song now) or cries for some technofix that will make all the horrible things go away. What matters most is the effect that the threat to nature has had on the vanguard of the environmental movement, who have rediscovered their kinship with the biosphere, mediated through kinships with various human groups. The children need a safe and healthy world to live in, just as we do. The larger community needs the ecosystems from which it draws its sustenance, or it will die. In the end, we are part of what Burch calls All Life, and the connection with All Life is powerful enough to become the ruling purpose of the lives of the ecowarriors of our time—the Rainbow Warriors, Sea Shepherds, and all the other varied groups who have found, in coming to the defense of the planet, that they have finally come home to their own families and their own selves.

> From this perspective, life itself has value, wilderness has value, and the human project finds its meaning by situating itself seamlessly *within* the community of All Life that inhabits the planet as a whole. The goal of human existence is not, as practiced by the culture of consumerism, simply to *expand* through physical growth until every nook and cranny of the Earth is filled with something made or discarded by humans. Rather, the goal of human existence is to *deepen consciousness* of our place in All Life and to develop a greater capacity for *love,* or *compassion,* or *holiness*—whatever word we wish to use to describe the realization of the transcendent possibilities of human existence . . .within All Life.[34]

This passage is atypically mystical for a very practical work. But the point is clear. There is a life in the universe of which our lives are small parts. In order to live our lives authentically, we have to conform them somehow to this larger scheme of life. When we have done that, we find that we are part of its life, as are the various human communities of which we are a part. The conforming exercise is the stripping of extraneous desires, tendencies, and "stuff" until we get close to the simple life. At that point, living in tune with the natural environment—living sustainably—we become part of its life. And when that happens, the experience is as one of joy, deep consciousness, or love. Sustaining the environment demands the simple life, and living the simple life is in itself a conscious and deliberate act of protecting the environment.

RESPONSIBILITY

Happiness, according to Aristotle (see Chapter 1) is activity of soul in accordance with virtue, and if there be several virtues, then with the highest and best. There are many environmental virtues, as Chapter 1 pointed out: wisdom, courage (patience), temperance, justice, curiosity, humility, and simplicity were all mentioned. But the highest and best is simplicity, which alone has the range to integrate a whole and fulfilled human life with a sustained effort to protect the environment. The fulfilled human life incorporates the worldview of stewardship—responsibility for self, family, community, nation, and the natural world on which these are based. In determining the way the simple life is lived in current conditions, we may adapt the method of the end of Chapter 1, describing the good life as a series of concentric circles of obligation, but informed further with the centrality of the notion of simplicity, as sketched in the last section.

Responsibility for the Self

First we have to deal with ourselves. As above, our choice of the way to live must be conditioned not on what would be great if everyone did it, but on what would be great if we were the only ones in the world doing it. There is no day but today, no life but mine, that I can live. By this point in the argument, the good life for me, for the individual, becomes evident in three phases, or moments.

As described in Chapter 1 (following Aristotle, Book I of the *Nicomachean Ethics*), virtue is developed in the individual by simple habit. There is no way to do this save by the establishment of good laws, uniform enforcement of those laws by reward for obedience as well as by punishment for deviation, capped by instruction on the reasons for those laws so that they may become part of the individual's deliberate intentions. Phase One of the exercise of responsibility for the self is, paradoxically, totally outside the control of the self: we must be born into a society that supplies not only the physical basics of life, but also the institutional basis for the good life, in solid institutions embodying good rules. This point underscores the conclusion of Chapter 1, that there is no way the individual can consistently will his own good without simultaneously willing the good of the community in which he grows.

This is also why we seem to be asking for trouble if we raise our children in cultures that we do not, ultimately, want them to assimilate. If we want our children to learn to play the piano, they must practice the right notes; if we want them to play good tennis, they must practice the right strokes; no parent needs to be told that. If we want our children to appreciate the life of simplicity, we must raise them in it. There is no substitute for correct practice in acquiring good habits, and there is no substitute for requiring correct practice in transmitting to the child the importance that the parent attaches to the virtue acquired. Why do we rail against television, video games, fast food, and then raise our children with them? It would seem that, being raised on video games and fast foods of which parents uproariously disapprove, the children would have to acquire habits of playing video games, eating fast food, and ignoring parents. It has been argued that no culture before ours has paid so little attention to socializing its children into its moral tradition; it will be a long time before the results of this inattention are fully known.

Suppose it all comes out right. Having acquired the habits of industriousness, temperance, and courage that will last a life long, the person must go on to learn the reasons for the habits already learned. At this point, the second phase of the moral development of the person, the moral life becomes reflective. This change is not optional. As noted in Chapter 1, Aristotle reaches his definition of "happiness," the description of the good human life, by determining the unique ability of humans—the ability to reason—and proceeding from that point to conclude that the good human life must be lived by deliberation and choice. (Just as we can tell by inspection of the animal in question that fish must swim and birds must fly to live fulfilled lives, just so we can tell that humans will not live fully human lives unless they themselves choose that life.) If the life is not reasoned and chosen, the life is not human.

The third phase of the moral life is outlined in the preceding section under the heading of "vocation." Rationality permits many human lives—indeed, an infinite number of good, virtuous, and joyful human lives, complete in themselves and serving the community. But each human being can only live one of them. The discernment of vocation is the search conducted by each human being to find that one which is uniquely fitted for him.

Christians decided early what the Greeks had already known, that the full life must be lived in community, and that, in that sense, it made little sense to speak of a life lived well alone. Yet solitude is an option worth considering. Generations of religious hermits have explored and perfected the simple life lived alone. It is a life of quiet routine, minimizing activity and consumption of material goods, focused on the living out of some task (like writing, prayer, gardening, or some combination of them) so that the physical aspect of the life can be seen as only a means to the completion of a fully human spiritual life. It would not necessarily be a life of true physical isolation, although that is possible. There is a long and noble tradition of those who chose life completely alone, like the Desert Fathers early in the Christian tradition, to avoid any contamination from the world. (Even they, like Thoreau, entertained visitors.) A step from such a hermit's life was the rule of certain monasteries, where the monks would gather only for certain tasks or events. What is morally important is not so much the sheer quantity of solitude, but its availability to be a part of a moral life.

It could be argued that every moral life should have solitude available as part of it. Solitude can play a series of roles in the moral life. It can initiate moral reflection, rather as Thoreau used it. A solitary "retreat," allowing the person to confront himself without the jangle of the world around, may be a crucial time of reflection and redirection. It may be essential to realizing spiritual potential. Aristotle, in the ninth book of the *Nicomachean Ethics*, argues that self-love, the fulfillment of the self, is fundamental to all morality as the basis of all friendship.[35] He goes on, in the tenth book, to suggest that the life that transcends all social duties and roles may be the highest life of which the human being is capable.[36] The religious traditions have put a sharper point on Aristotle's aspiration: We came into this world alone, and will leave it alone, and must face our Creator alone. No community can substitute for the examined individual life.

The Community: Family, Village, and *Polis*

For social species, designed by nature to be engaged with others, the life most under consideration is the life with others. Aristotle, whom we have followed throughout, sketches the central types of human community, under the general headings of household, village, and *polis*, city-state, in the second chapter of the first book of the *Politics*. He starts with a hypothetical individual, and rapidly concludes that this individual will have to form relationships with others—with a woman, and with a slave—in order to live. From these two relationships he generates, respectively, family and property (which the slaves help him to accumulate and work). Together, these two form the household, essentially an institution for the material maintenance of the members of it. No higher goal is given it, and from our experience, that's about all it can manage. It is not self-sufficient.

The "village," as Aristotle describes it, grows naturally out of the household, and sustains it. It is a kinship-linked bearer of the history of the family-clan, a family of enough significance to have a story to tell, of the gods and their role in the founding of the family, of the wealth and victory that has allowed them to survive, of the special obligations and laws that were given them by their gods as a condition of further protection. The village, or tribe or nation, is illustrated for us in the Hebrew Scriptures, since the nation of the Jews, from Egypt to the present day, operated as such a God-founded congregation. Unlike the household, which perishes with the death of its head, the village or tribe is immortal; as long as there are members who carry on the culturally prescribed laws, the tribe lives. Under the heading of "culture," we understand not only art and music, but language, economic institutions, and above all the narrative history of the tribe, describing the relations among gods, humans, and the natural world that the gods have given the humans. In these narratives, we find the seeds of ecological consciousness that can blossom at some point when the group has the leisure to set aside the pursuit of material goods. Thus the Native Americans of our time, achieving a moment of sufficiency, if not prosperity, can take the lead in reminding us of our obligations to the natural environment.

Aristotle conceived of the state, or *polis,* as essentially different from the village. The village could of course grow into a state, in the course of nature, but by the time it got there, it would have a wholly different form of operation, just because of its size. No longer would the tradition of the tribal religion be sufficient to govern a much larger and more diverse collection of people. We need formal laws, courts, assemblies to debate the issues of the day, formal votes, and a system of officials who attend to governing full time.

By tradition, the state does not grow from a single village, but is established by a free decision of the tribes that make it up. No tribe can renounce the authority of its history, gods, and laws, the reasoning goes, so when necessity (the threat of foreign invasion, most likely) dictates the merger of the tribes into some larger entity, that entity has to work according to very different laws and principles. It cannot import the detailed kin-based hierarchy of the tribe, since no tribe will consent to have its members treated as inferiors by members of any other tribe; therefore the equality of the Citizen was created. It cannot import wholesale the authority structures and laws of any one of the tribes, so it has to devise its own, and no mechanism exists save the consent of the citizens. Because the authority of the government offices surely feels like rulership, to its occupants and to those governed by them, and because no tribe can consent to be ruled indefinitely by members of any other tribe, the only way the government can work is by having the citizens rule and be ruled in turn—sometimes literally taking turns in state office, sometimes chosen by lot, sometimes elected by a vote of the whole citizenry. In the *polis*, as Aristotle describes it, we have the perfect home for the human being. The human must live his life rationally, by deliberation and choice, and the *polis*, lacking the natural authority of the head of the family or the traditional authority of the tribal council, must be governed by collective deliberation and choice. The *polis* therefore becomes the perfect teacher of rational deliberation for the growing student, and the natural outlet for the deliberations of rational citizens trying to govern themselves according to what is useful and what is just. Aristotle demonstrated through several lines of argument that the *polis* was natural, and the natural home of the human being (as the hive is the natural home of the bee). Nature makes nothing in vain, for instance; and nature has given humans language, a means of communication capable of balancing abstract concepts, just what humans need who must debate the nature of the common good and the equitable law. But the central argument is inescapable, and valid: The *polis* is the context of life according to collective deliberation and choice, mirroring the life of the rational individual.

The communities—household, village, and *polis*—are distinguished one from another by their ends, or goals, *teloi*. The household aims at the day-to-day nurturing of its members; the resources of the whole are available to each. The village protects a culture, a tradition, for the sake of which individuals may be sacrificed—literally, or lost in war. If they are not physically sacrificed, their interests and drive for individual fulfillment may be set aside to maintain room for the larger interests of the culture. The *polis*, as serving the whole interest of the human being, can rightfully demand his entire service, in the economy, in military service, and in government.

Note the beauty, and clarity, of Aristotle's schema. For the creation of laws so just that the polity becomes a loyal and hard-working people willing to govern and be governed in turn, the lawmaker is justly praised. In creating just institutions, the lawmaker may be credited with the creation of a just people. (George Will, in *Statecraft as Soulcraft*, argued powerfully that the central duty of a government is the shaping of the moral character of its citizens.[37])

Above all, the natural communities are arenas for the exercise of responsibility. Humans will not survive without care and nurturing. The first requirement of such care is in the household. The household Aristotle conceived primarily biologically, but with allowance for many non-family members who would be part of it. It is particularly interesting that in Book I of the *Politics*, Aristotle continues his discussion of the household with an extended discussion of slaves and our duties to them. Why slaves? Because they are persons whose lives are so defined that they will not have any dealings with anyone outside the household; their lives are confined within it. Therefore they will never know any goal higher than, or different from, the nurturing of the individuals they serve. Households are defined the same way today. They are no longer only biological. We have learned to extend that notion to any group arrangement whose primary end is to nurture its members through the ministrations of a community—including, as an excellent example of the type, the "group home" for the mentally incapacitated.

The village is the primary community, any natural neighborhood or any deliberate re-creation of the now non-existent neighborhood, physically (through gathering into an intentional community), virtually (on the Internet), or any other way. In Aristotle's understanding, that the village lives not for its members but for its story—its history, tradition, religion, unique culture—we find the difference between the 1960s communes that made it and those that did not. Those that attempted to operate as households, existing only to serve the needs and growth of individuals, failed, even as the household dissolves when the strong leadership that formed it weakens. Religious communities, or those formed to perpetuate any belief-system (including Skinner's behavioral psychology!) had a better chance of survival. Those that had a Rule, requiring certain kinds of simplicity, radically increased their chance of making it. In short, where there was a culture, a tradition, a collective identity that transcended the individuals, the individuals did better in community and for themselves.

The *polis* is the ultimate locus for the exercise of responsibility. The governing citizen, especially the citizen currently holding office, bears on his shoulders the responsibility for the decisions that may result in the death of all the citizens (if he misreads a military move on the part of an enemy), or worse yet, destroy its freedom. For the greatest achievement of the *polis* (according to Hannah Arendt, in *On Revolution*) is its creation of a public space, historically associated with the marketplace, or *agora* (literally field, open place), in which political dialogue, policy deliberation, was protected, and could become law and policy. The creation of the constitutional structure to protect that dialogue she called the "establishment of liberty," and it is possible only when history and geography have combined to provide a nation with a unique chance to consider how it shall be governed. It does not happen often, and is supremely worthy of protection when it does.[38]

The search for political simplicity can be read in part as an attempt to re-create that *polis*. The political movements, too, succeeded or failed to the extent that they realized that responsibility. To the extent that they took as their primary objective the nurturing of a public space, they tended to settle into the political entities that already existed (incorporated towns and villages), and disappeared from any "alternative living" scheme as they succeeded in re-energizing their own local governments. Success in politics took them out of the national press entirely—as it should.

Where they failed, their failure is instructive. The political "communes," formed for single political purposes to thwart some outside political force, or achieve some agenda within the larger political entity, acquired a strange and new social pathology as the political scene changed. To the extent that they were energized by hostility to larger political entities, not by any vision of themselves, they should logically have dissolved when the larger entities changed—when the Vietnam engagement ended, when the civil rights movement achieved the bulk of its objectives. But logic is not the whole story of a community. The political work they had been doing, the shared tasks, the encouragement of their colleagues, the joyful union in struggle and accomplishment, turns out to be intensely rewarding in itself, not just as accomplishing some pre-set task. So they stayed together, fragments of the "anti-war" movement pawing around for some new cause that could provide the same rewards. Often, as with the "infant formula" controversy, they simply adapted scraps of political and professional disagreements to the purposes of a new "Movement," and continued their organizing and publicizing work as usual. The result of this transformation has been the creation of a new category of "not-for-profit" organizations—the all-purpose activists, ready to take a position (anti-government and anti-corporation) on a wide variety of issues, quick with the banners, news conferences, public demonstrations, and violent "actions" against people and property. Parasitic on the news media, they cannot survive without something to oppose and without official condemnation by some part of the political and corporate establishment; they cannot survive without sowing division wherever they act. And by now, survival has come to seem the supreme value for them. One agenda of the postmodern world is the determination of the place of these organizations in the general polity.

We have taken on, in this section, no lighter a question than the achievement of the good life for the human community, at least on the small scale. The answer is deceptively simple: Find a society in which the life of simplicity can be lived, or create one. The answer also satisfies some of the deepest questions of traditional ethical theories. It explains J. S. Mill's insistence that even as we seek our own "happiness," nevertheless this search (contrary to experience) includes each person's desire to improve his own character. While "desiring the improvement of our own character" may be a difficult notion to encompass, there is nothing difficult in desiring the achievement of a society whose chief duty and activity is nurturing citizens of good character. That society accomplishes the work that we as humans need done, at all levels, and it turns out to be the happiest society to live in, in any case. This answer also satisfies Kant's vision of a "Kingdom of Ends," of which we aim to be full legislative members, for it requires the moral agent to engage that agency in the collective deliberation and choice of the political workings of a nation of such agents. Such is the good society. We know, at least in outline, how to bring about this society. Implementation turns out to be full of difficulties, most of which, thankfully, are beyond the scope of this essay. In the next section we will conclude the survey of the responsible life by tying it back into the biosphere from which we came.

Responsibility for Nature

If we are morally obligated to assume responsibility as the central characteristic of our moral lives, and if the discernment of the scope of that responsibility is based in part on recognition of our dependence on the communities of which we form a part, then responsibility cannot stop with the human, but must incorporate the biosphere as well. What would the sustainable life entail?

First, to put the matter in the Aristotelian progression, there is the habituation to a life that makes no more demands on the planet than it must, and gives back what it can. That rule requires that instead of helping the developing nations to live at the level of the average North American (which will unfortunately require 16 additional planets in less than 30 years!), we find the simplest standard of living at which material needs are met. Nakedness and firesticks are not required. A simple decision not to buy more than a few sets of clothes, to use the fan for air conditioning, and to leave all possible electronic devices at the office, will drop your demands on the planet enormously. A decision not to eat beef will do the same, and prolong your life at the same time. But the point is not *this* renunciation, or *that* abstention. The point is that this is a more enjoyable life, because it is less burdened by things that must be expensively acquired, which drain the planet in their extraction and production, and then hang around, largely unneeded or positively harmful. When such a sustainable life becomes a habit, the roar of the half-conscious fantasies of multitudes of identities, along with the advertising that addresses them, fades away, and life becomes quiet.

Does this help the land? Yes, in a minuscule sort of way. It will not slow down the deterioration of the environment by one iota. Of course, if everyone did it, it would halt the devastation immediately, turn it around, and give nature a chance to recover. But everyone won't, as we know, so there's no point in thinking about that.

To accomplish any task of saving the land, the next Aristotelian step must be taken. The habituation must become rational. *Why* do we live simply, save every bit of trash for re-use or recycling, watch our purchases and watch our treatment of the land, especially when others do not? The education appropriate for sustainable life will parallel the education for social life. As social organisms, we must live in society, so we are first habituated to a life of fulfilling duties, then educated in ethics. As living organisms, we must live in the biosphere, All Life, and having first been habituated to living in accordance with its limits, we must then be educated to make that life rational and, no less important, teachable, transmissible, if only to our children. Education requires ecology, the science of life on earth, so that we will know the relationships between our behavior and the life of the planet, and it requires technology (the subject of Chapter 2), so that we will know the ways that we can nurture those relationships to our mutual benefit. In the current situation, more relations must be known. We must understand the workings of agriculture, mining, forestry, fishing, and all the industries that directly impinge on the land; we must understand the workings of business, economics, law, and politics, that purport to govern these industries for the common good; and we must understand the science of communications, for stewardship of the land will demand that we be effective in communicating to our fellow citizens. The point should be clear: In the category of simple survival, we ought to live the simple life in harmony with nature. But as rational beings, we are obliged to support the right relationship among humans and their natural ecosystems even as we are obliged to maintain a moral society. A kingdom of ends might very well include the land, at least as much an end in itself as any human being. That support will require teaching, demonstration, and political activity, to the extent that we are able to undertake it. There is no opting out.

Even as we are obliged to be rational and supportive members of a *polis*, active citizens of the political association, so we are called upon to be active, knowledgeable and persuasive citizens of the biosphere. But the third level of environmental citizenship, that of individual vocation, is open here as elsewhere. Burch recounts, with a kind of awe, the transformation of life experienced by the Sea Shepherds, dedicated to the protection of the whales and dolphins, or the members of Greenpeace who undertook to live in the forest they were trying to protect. He might have mentioned also "Leakey's Angels," the three primatologists (Jane Goodall, Dian Fossey, and Birute Galdikas), who went to the forests to study, as good scientists, the remaining species of great ape. As they interacted with their subjects (the better to "study" them), they became transformed from scientists to protectors. As their apes came under increasing pressure (in Africa, now, markets feature "bushmeat," with long arms and legs), the primatologists became more active in their defense and more pointed in their advocacy. At the end, Fossey was dead, killed by poachers; Goodall and Galdikas were spending most of their time raising money to expand the preserves in which they kept the apes they had managed to save from the hunters. The quest now consumes their whole lives, and they would not have it any other way. Apparently we need move only slightly into nature, to discover that it is our family, and to get caught up in its defense. But what life we lead in that defense is a matter of individual disposition, opportunity, and calling. The third phase of human growth, that of discerning an individual path in the sustainable life, must be determined by each individual in conversation with himself, with the natural world around him, and with whatever he takes to be God.

THE WORLDVIEW OF STEWARDSHIP

A steward is one who is entrusted with something. The steward's job is to protect it from loss or injury, care for it, enhance it if possible. Responsibility entails stewardship. Very well, with what have we been entrusted? We may take the list from the last section, for none of those objects of responsibility were made by us. We have first ourselves, our minds and our bodies, to take care of. Second, we have our families, our communities, our inheritances of culture and tradition. Third, we have our laws, the rights of citizens, courts, polity, and the whole infrastructure of freedom to protect. Fourth, we have the natural world to protect. All of these are so many manifestations of, shells of, houses of, the soul. They are all ours.

What does a responsible life look like? Let us return to the example of the Jonathan Foley family of Chapter 2. It may not seem that Foley is doing any extensive good, a limitation of which he is well aware. "He knows that the emissions of one family are a mere drop in the ocean of atmospheric pollution. But . . . he hopes that by modeling energy efficiency while maintaining a comfortable lifestyle, his family will see its actions ripple through the lives of students, neighbors, and colleagues. Indeed, it's the responsibility of a scientist to act on the results of his or her research, argues Foley. 'We can't hide out in an ivory tower anymore.'" There is a ripple there; there is some evidence that the Foley family's choices are having some effect on their neighbors.[39] But that's not really the point. The point is that what he does, he does for good, and whatever difference he makes, is positive. Living a good life needs no further consequences.

Let us end the discussion of stewardship with a final quote from Juergen Schrempp, chairman of the board of DaimlerChrysler. Remember the fuel cells of Chapter 2? In the recent financial reverses of DaimlerChrysler, there has been talk of cutting costs across the board. Yet Schrempp is protecting the fuel cell program's $1 billion line of credit. He explains why in a recent speech to the World Engineers Convention, where "the engineer-turned-business leader implored engineers around the world" to throw down their projects and jump on the fuel cell bandwagon. Schrempp's rationale? Ensuring that future generations are not overwhelmed by global climate change and economic dislocations from declining oil supplies. "We all share the responsibility for carrying out this project, for the assumption of responsibility is part of the dignity of human beings."[40]

NOTES

[1]Paul Hawken, Amory Lovins, and L. Hunter Lovins, *Natural Capitalism*, Boston: Little, Brown & Company, 1999, p. 207 Emphasis supplied.

[2]Ibid. p. 212. Emphasis supplied

[3]Fyodor Dostoevsky, *Notes from Underground*, selections, in Walter Kaufmann, ed., *Existentialism from Dostoevsky to Sartre*, New York: NAL, 1975, p. 67.

[4]There are advertisements where the word "intimidation" is specifically used to describe the SUV's advantages. Sometimes it gets out of hand: James Cobb, commenting on a new luxury SUV, the 285–horsepower Chevy Avalanche 2002, wonders why the vehicle advertises "aggressive rubber floor mats." "With all the talk about road rage, do we really need attitude in our floor coverings?" James G. Cobb, "Ride 'em, Urban Cowboy," *The New York Times*, July 29, 2001, Automobiles (section 12), p. 1.

[5]A bibliography could follow at this point. See at least the essays in the fine anthology, *Ethics of Consumption: The Good Life, Justice, and Global Stewardship*, edited by David Crocker and Toby Linden, New York: Rowman and Littlefield, 1998. The prophetic howls of horrified observers of the moral scene rise from every page of the popular press, continually new, continually appalled. See (for instance) Alan Wolfe, "The Final Freedom," a discourse on "moral freedom," in *The New York Times Magazine*, March 18, 2001, pp. 48 ff., or Lewis H. Lapham, "Notebook: Mirror, Mirror on the Wall," a discourse on materialism and greed, in *Harpers Magazine*, April 2001, pp. 12 ff.

[6]St. Vincent de Paul, *Elevations, Prieres, et Pensees*, cited in S. J. Raoul Plus, *Simplicity*, Westminster, MD: The Newman Press, 1951, p. 16.

[7]Plus, pp. 17–18.

[8]"To order your life as you desire you must know how to conquer yourself." St. Ignatius, cited in Plus, p. 20.

[9]Ibid., pp. 21–23.

[10]Ibid., pp. 28–29.

[11]Duane Elgin, *Voluntary Simplicity*, New York: Morrow, 1993, pp. 123–127.

[12]This account of the notion of "vocation" is adapted from several sources, but relies most immediately on Parker J. Palmer, *Let Your Life Speak: Listening for the Voice of Vocation*, San Francisco: Jossey Bass, 2000. Quote from p. 6.

[13]Ibid, p. 11, citing Martin Buber, *Tales of the Hasidim: The Early Masters*, New York: Schocken Books, 1975, p. 251.

[14]Ibid. p. 16, citing Frederick Buechner, *Wishful Thinking: A Seeker's ABC*, San Francisco: Harper San Francisco, 1993, p. 119.

[15]Elgin, *Voluntary Simplicity*, pp. 134–135.

[16]Ibid. p. 140.

[17]Robert Ellsberg, "St. Benedict, Monk," *All Saints*, New York: Crossroad Publishing Company, 1998, pp. 297–298.

[18]Palmer, *Let Your Life Speak*, p. 17.

[19]Kathleen Kinkade, *A Walden II Experiment: The First Five Years of Twin Oaks Community* (1973); Twin Oaks webpage www.twinoaks.org

[20]Adam Daniel Finnerty, *No More Plastic Jesus: Global Justice and Christian Lifestyle*, 2nd ed., Maryknoll, NY: Orbis Books, 1977.

[21]Finnerty, p. 99.

[22]Palmer, p. 32.

[23]Janice Castro, "The Simple Life," *TIME*, cover story, April 1991. Available on internet at time.com.

[24]Rebecca Winters, "Did They Find a Simple Life? It's Complicated," *TIME*, April 16, 2001, p. 4.

[25]Castro, "The Simple Life.".

[26]Ibid.

[27]Ibid.

[28]Mark A. Burch, *Stepping Lightly: Simplicity for People and the Planet*, Gabriola Island, B.C.: New Society Publishers, 2000, pp. 27–29, citing Joe Dominguez and Vicki Robin, *Your Money Or Your Life: Transforming Your Relationship With Money and Achieving Financial Independence*, New York: Penguin, 1992.

[29]Burch, p. 34.

[30]Mathis Wackernagel and William Rees, *Our Ecological Footprint: Reducing Human Impact on the Earth*, Gabriola Island, BC: New Society Publishers, 1995.

[31]Burch, p. 79.

[32]Burch, p. 80.

[33]Burch, p. 80.

[34]Burch, pp. 82–83.

[35]Aristotle, *Nicomachean Ethics*, Book IX, chapter 4, Martin Ostwald, ed., New York: Macmillan, 1962, pp. 252–253.

[36]Book X, Chapter 8, ibid. pp. 293–294.

[37]George F. Will, *Statecraft as Soulcraft: What Government Does*, New York: Simon & Schuster, 1983.

[38]Hannah Arendt, *On Revolution*, New York: Viking Press, 1965, Chapter 4.

[49]Brian Lavendel, "GreenHouse," *Audubon*, March–April 2001, p. 77

[40]Peter Fairley, "Fill 'er Up with Hydrogen," *Technology Today*, November–December 2000, p. 62.

BIBLIOGRAPHY

Arendt, Hannah, *On Revolution*, New York: Viking Press, 1965.

Buber, Martin, *Tales of the Hasidim: The Early Masters*, New York: Schocken Books, 1975.

Buechner, Frederick, *Wishful Thinking: A Seeker's ABC*, San Francisco: Harper San Francisco, 1993.

Burch, Mark A., *Stepping Lightly: Simplicity for People and the Planet*, Gabriola Island, B.C.: New Society Publishers, 2000.

Castro, Janice "The Simple Life," *TIME* cover story, April 1991. Available on internet at time.com.

Cobb, James G., "Ride 'em, Urban Cowboy," *The New York Times*, July 29, 2001, Automobiles (section 12) p. 1.

Crocker, David and Toby Linden, eds., *Ethics of Consumption: The Good Life, Justice, and Global Stewardship*, New York: Rowman and Littlefield, 1998.

Dominguez, Joe, and Vicki Robin, *Your Money Or Your Life: Transforming Your Relationship With Money and Achieving Financial Independence*, New York: Penguin, 1992.

Dostoevsky, Fyodor, *Notes from Underground*, selections, in Walter Kaufmann, ed., *Existentialism from Dostoevskv to Sartre*, New York: NAL, 1975.

Elgin, Duane, *Voluntary Simplicity*, New York: Morrow, 1993.

Ellsberg, Robert, *All Saints*, New York: Crossroad Publishing Company, 1998.

Finnerty, Adam Daniel, *No More Plastic Jesus: Global Justice and Christian Lifestyle*, 2nd ed., Maryknoll, NY: Orbis Books, 1977.

Fogler, Michael, *Un-Jobbing: The Adult Liberation Handbook*, 2nd ed., Lexington, KY: Free Choice Press, 1999.

Kinkade, Kathleen, *A Walden Two Experiment: The First Five Years of Twin Oaks Community*, foreword by B. F. Skinner. New York: Morrow, 1973.

Lapham, Lewis H., "Notebook: Mirror, Mirror on the Wall," *Harpers Magazine*, April 2001, pp. 12ff.

Plus, Raoul S. J., *Simplicity*, Westminster, MD: The Newman Press, 1951.

Segal, Jerome M., *Graceful Simplicity: Toward a Philosophy and Politics of Simple Living*, New York: Henry Holt & Co., 1999.

Wackemagel, Mathis and William Rees, *Our Ecological Footprint: Reducing Human Impact on the Earth*, Gabriola Island, B.C.: New Society Publishers, 1995.

Will, George F., *Statecraft as Soulcraft: What Government Does*, New York: Simon & Schuster, 1983.

Winters, Rebecca, "Did They Find a Simple Life? It's Complicated," *TIME*, April 16, 2001, p. 4.

Wolfe, Alan, "The Final Freedom," *The New York Times Magazine*, March 18, 2001, pp. 48 ff.

Index